WILD
FLOWERS
OF KENYA & NORTHERN TANZANIA

Anne Powys

T0351856

Published by Struik Nature
(an imprint of Penguin Random House South Africa (Pty) Ltd)
Reg. No. 1953/000441/07
The Estuaries No. 4, Oxbow Crescent
Century Avenue, Century City, 7441
PO Box 1144, Cape Town, 8000 South Africa

Visit www.struiknature.co.za and join the Struik
Nature Club for updates, news, events and special offers.

First published in 2019 by Struik Nature

10 9 8 7 6 5 4 3 2

Publisher: Pippa Parker
Managing editor: Helen de Villiers
Editor: Emily Donaldson
Designer: Gillian Black
Proofreader: Thea Grobbelaar

Reproduction by Hirt & Carter Cape (Pty) Ltd
Printed and bound in China by RR Donnelley

Print: 9781775842453
E-pub: 9781775842460

Front cover: *Abutilon hirtum;* back cover (top): *Boophone disticha;*
back cover (centre): *Impatiens tinctoria* (BCa)*;* back cover (bottom): *Asystasia guttata;*
page 1: *Nymphaea lotus* (AR); page 3: *Desmidorchis speciosa* (NP)

Key to photographers' initials
AC Abigail Church; **AR** Ann Robertson; **AV** Archie Voorspuy; **BCa** Barry Cameron;
BC Bob Campbell; **BL** Belinda Levitan; **BOT** Botbln/WC/CC BY-SA 3.0; **BVW** Braam van
Wyk; **CN** Catherine Ngarachu; **CTJ** CT Johansson/WC/CC BY-SA 3.0; **DM** Dino Martins;
DR Dee Roberts; **FKS** Forest & Kim Starr/WC/CC BY 3.0; **FV** Frank Vincentz/WC/ CC
BY-SA 3.0; **HS** Helmut Steiner; **KB** Ken Brown; **KH** Kate Hewitt; **LG** Lourens Grobler;
LN Len Newton; **MR** Melissa Rotureau; **MS** Marco Schmidt/www.africanplants.
senckenberg.de; **MW** Michael Wolf/WC/CC BY 3.0; **MWS** Marian Wreford-Smith;
NP Nigel Pavitt; **PW** Peter Warren/iNaturalist/public domain; **SA** Sue Allen;
SP Stickpen/WC/public domain

CONTENTS

ACKNOWLEDGEMENTS AND DEDICATION

With this pocket guide I hope to inspire people to get outside and see what's around them, whether it be on the verge of a main road or 4,000m up the slopes of Mt Kenya. To this end I have included a broad range of flowers – from the widespread and commonly encountered, to those that occur only in very remote areas. Without the fabulous photographs of the following contributors it wouldn't have been possible to represent such a diversity of flowering plants.

Special thanks must go to the following who contributed their photographs to the project: Dee Roberts, Belinda Levitan, Nigel Pavitt, Ann Robertson, Archie Voorspuy, Abigail Church, my sister Marian, Barry Cameron, Sue Allen, Catherine Ngarachu, Kate Hewett, Melissa Rotureau, Len Newton and Dino Martins.

A special thank you to Len Newton who also agreed to look over the book before going to print – a huge task and one we are so grateful for.

Thanks to Quentin Luke for taking so much time to check all the photos and text and to Catherine Ngarachu for all your encouragement. Your lovely bird book and Dino's butterfly and dudu books were a great inspiration. Lissa Ruben – huge appreciation for taking me up and down the coast to look for flowers to photograph.

To my son Ciaran – thank you for your useful suggestions on getting information across in a simple, accessible way, for checking all the text, and for helping me to keep this project alive against the odds. Thanks also to my parents, Gilfrid and Patricia, both completely at home in nature, whose knowledge of plants has had a profound impact on my life.

A final thank you must go to three very special ladies at Struik Nature – Pippa Parker, I am extremely grateful to you for giving me the opportunity to put together such an important pocket guide, and to Emily Donaldson and Gillian Black for contending with many 'waits' to receive material. Thank you all for your extraordinary patience and understanding throughout the project.

Dedicated to my father Gilfrid Powys (79), who was killed by an elephant on Suyian Ranch on 27 December 2017. He spent much of his life ranching and exploring the plants of East Africa. Among his wonderful collection of plants are several newly discovered and undescribed species. He was an inspiration to me and I'm forever grateful for his spirit of adventure.

Acanthus eminens

INTRODUCTION

Blessed with a rich diversity of habitats, Kenya and northern Tanzania boast thousands of flowering plants. In selecting the 400 species for this guide, an attempt has been made to include wild flowers from all of these habitats and to include not only those that are frequently encountered, bold and unmistakable, but also the small wayside flowers that may be well hidden in thick vegetation and difficult to track down (even in the existing literature!).

Some invasive or 'weedy' species have also been included here. Whether we like it or not, a 'pristine' environment is little more than a myth today. Agriculture, pastoralism and rapid expansion of urban areas mean that many species are now found in areas where they did not originally occur.

Generally it is exotics that become a nuisance, but there are several indigenous flowers, climbers and succulent plants that may be considered weeds. It's been said that a weed is simply 'a plant whose virtues have yet to be discovered' and indeed, there is always a reason why an indigenous wild plant starts behaving in a 'weedy' way. Usually the ground has been disturbed, overused, sprayed with chemicals or overgrazed. 'Weeds' may appear to be taking over, when in fact they are simply pioneer species covering damaged, lifeless areas. In time, other plants establish themselves and, in due course, nature restores the habitat to its original state of health and biodiversity.

Vegetation zones of Kenya and northern Tanzania

Flower species tend to occur within, and be adapted for, life in specific vegetation zones. Kenya and northern Tanzania have many such zones, but for the purposes of this book the most important types are forest, grassland and bushland, and these are briefly described below.

Note that wild flowers are typically seen in December/January, following the short rains of November/December. They're also present in June, after the long rains, which occur in April/May.

Moist forest

Dry cedar-olive forest

Wooded grassland

Open grassland

Forest

- **Moist forest** occurs at high altitude, in areas that receive approximately 1,500mm of rain annually. Key species are *Hagenia abyssinica*, *Juniperus procera*, *Olea europea* subsp. *cuspidatus*, *Afrocarpus gracilior* and *Afriocarpus latifolius*. This forest type is typical of Mt Kenya, the Southern Mau, the Aberdares, Mt Meru and Mt Kilimanjaro.
- **Dry forest** occurs at lower altitude and experiences distinct dry seasons. It is less diverse than the moist forest type. The most common large trees include *Croton megalocarpus*, *Juniperus procera*, *Afrocarpus gracilior*, *Olea europea* subsp. *cuspidatus* and *Ficus thonningii*. Trees typical of the understorey are *Vepris simplicifolia*, *Ehretia cymosa* and *Strychnos mitis*.

Grassland

- **Wooded grassland** can consist either of stretches of open grassland with some scattered trees, or of small groups of trees spread throughout a rather flat, grassy landscape. Typical species include acacias such as *Acacia drepanolobium* and *Acacia gerrardii*.
- **Open grassland** consists almost exclusively of grasses, with trees and bushes comprising less than 10% of the total area. Soils tend be shallow, overlying rock, or there may be large areas of clay-like black cotton soils that are waterlogged for long periods.

Bushed grassland

■ **Bushed grassland** comprises grasses interspersed with shrubs or trees below 6m, such as *Carissa edulis*, *Rhus natalensis* and *Grewia* species. This vegetation type is often found on quite rocky terrain.

Acacia-Commiphora bushland

Bushland

■ ***Acacia-Commiphora* bushland** covers extensive semi-arid areas including Mkomazi, Tsavo East, and much of northern Kenya. *Acacia* and *Commiphora* species tend to be the dominant trees.

Acacia bushland

■ ***Acacia* bushland** occurs at moderate altitude, in areas receiving up to 450mm of rain annually. *Acacia*, *Rhus* and *Vepris* species predominate, especially in rocky areas. *Commiphora* species are absent.

■ **Coastal bushland** has a canopy of thick evergreen shrubs, interspersed with some taller trees. This vegetation type is typical of undisturbed habitats close to the sea and the adjacent coastal belt.

Coastal bushland

Pollination

Not only are plants adapted to the vegetation zone in which they occur, they're also adapted to lure pollinators. The relationships between plants and these vital visitors are wonderfully diverse and can be highly rewarding to observe. They also shed light on the reasons for the great variety of flower shapes and forms.

Many flowers have pollination adaptions such as spots or lines on their petals. These function, like the markings on an airstrip, to guide insects in search of nectar or pollen. On the 'landing pad' you might also notice grooves, ribs or hairs, which provide a stable surface on which the insect can balance while it forages. The genus *Ceropegia* has evolved a clever method of luring small flies down the floral tube. The inner tube is lined with small, stiff hairs that face downward. The fly can push its way forward but cannot return until the job is done. Only then do the hairs relax, allowing the small fly to emerge.

Pollination may depend on deception: *Eulophia* orchids, for example, do not produce nectar. Rather, they have evolved colourful flowers to 'seduce' pollinators into visiting and carrying away pollen. Tough-looking *Euphorbia* species produce nectar from flower-like structures called 'cyathia'. This nectar may be a lifesaver for pollinating bees and other insects during the dry season. (The resulting honey has a chilli-like taste and is a helpful treatment for sore throats.)

In East Africa the days are generally very hot and sunny. Many flowers have evolved to open for pollination in the mornings and close during the hottest hours of the day to protect themselves from the heat. In semi-arid and desert areas flowers are often white with a long floral tube. These plants are pollinated mainly by hawk moths during the cooler evening hours. Their white petals are conspicuous in the dark and they often release an attractive sweet scent, while the long floral tube conforms to the length of a hawk moth's proboscis.

Succulents in the genus *Desmidorchis* have developed a different pollination strategy: instead of releasing sweet perfume, the flowers give off the odour of rotting flesh. This attracts the bluebottle fly, a dry-climate carrion feeder.

Birds are also significant pollinators that have evolved along with particular flowers to their mutual benefit. For example, the Purple Sunbird has developed a shorter beak, instead of the typical long, curved beak of an upland sunbird. This beak is specifically suited to the flowers it feeds on, such as aloes and dryland parasites in the family Loranthaceae.

There is much more to be discovered about the pollinators of flowering plants, so it's worth taking some time to observe when you are out in the bush: you may well witness something that has never been seen before.

A female Eastern Violet-backed Sunbird dusted in pollen after feeding from a flowering *Aloe*

Identifying wild flowers using this book

This guide is organised into six colour groups. Within each, flowers are arranged alphabetically by family, and then alphabetically by species. Size, given after the family name in each account, is an indication of the average height of the plant. Brief text describes the features of the plant and flowers that will aid identification.

   To identify a wild flower, start by noting the colour of the petals and find the corresponding colour section of the book. Also make a note of the plant's overall size and shape, the arrangement of flowers on the stems, the leaf shape, and any unusual textures (e.g. hairiness or stickiness). You may not always find the exact species you have observed, but you may discover a related plant in the family group, which shares similar features to your specimen.

   Note: The classification and naming of plants is always in a state of flux, so for many species, older synonyms are given in brackets after the scientific name.

Illustrated glossary of leaf and flower parts and shapes

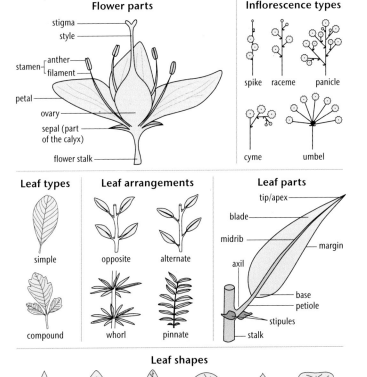

Flower parts

stigma
style
stamen — anther — filament
petal
ovary
sepal (part of the calyx)
flower stalk

Inflorescence types

spike   raceme   panicle

cyme   umbel

Leaf types

simple

compound

Leaf arrangements

opposite   alternate

whorl   pinnate

Leaf parts

tip/apex
blade
midrib
margin
axil
base
petiole
stipules
stalk

Leaf shapes

lanceolate   ovate   elliptical   round   triangular   wedge

Asystasia charmian
ACANTHACEAE FAMILY
50cm ◇ perennial

Habitat Dry *Acacia* bushland.
Identification An upright herb or small shrub, with rounded, lanceolate, slightly hairy leaves. The flowers are alternately arranged at the top of a 10cm stem. The interior of each flower is marked with purple spots and stripes **(1)**, and the 3cm-long flower tube **(2)** is softly hairy. The seeds are borne in a woody capsule.

Asystasia gangetica
ACANTHACEAE FAMILY
50cm ◇ perennial

Habitat Coastal bushland.
Identification This low-growing herb may cover large areas after the rains. It has squarish stems that root at the nodes, and broad, hairless leaves. Five-petalled flowers are arranged alternately along the stem and vary greatly in colour, from white to pale pink or deep pink, depending on the soil. The seed pods **(1)** are long, hairy, woody capsules that split in two when dry.

Asystasia mysorensis
ACANTHACEAE FAMILY
7cm ◇ annual

Habitat Forest margins at moderate to low altitude.
Identification A hairy herb that can be quite common in suitable habitat. It spreads out in shady areas. The leaves are broad but significantly smaller than those of *A. gangetica*. The small tubular flowers, up to 0.8cm long, are white with some green spots on the inner petals. The bracts **(1)** are large and pointed.

Barleria robertsoniae
ACANTHACEAE FAMILY
1m ◇ perennial

Habitat Dry bushland and grassland, within the shelter of a shrub or rocky outcrop.
Identification A straggly herb, this *Barleria* often uses other plants for support. The stem is clothed in downward-pointing hairs. The leaves are opposite, hairy and rounded; they may be up to 5cm long, but are generally smaller. The white flowers have four upper petals, a solitary lower petal **(1)**, a 6cm-long tube **(2)**, and deep purple hairs in the throat. The seeds are borne in a two-sided capsule.

Barleria submollis
ACANTHACEAE FAMILY
1m ◇ perennial

Habitat Open grassland and *Acacia* bushland.
Identification This herb is tall or spreading, with hairy stems that root along the nodes. The leaves are small and broadly ovate. It bears tubular flowers up to 4cm in length (smaller than those of *B. robertsoniae*) and that vary from white to very pale blue.

Barleria trispinosa
ACANTHACEAE FAMILY
1m ◇ perennial

Habitat A lower-altitude *Barleria*, occurring in shallow soil, among short grasses.
Identification This rounded, thorny plant is well branched. Spines up to 3cm long form in groups of three at nodes among the leaves. The leaves are broadly elliptical, with short stalks. It bears pretty, trumpet-shaped flowers, up to 5cm long, with narrow white petals and a pale yellow throat. The sepals are ovate, with a pointed tip (1).
Notes A good source of fodder for camels. Black Rhino and Grevy's Zebra also feed on this plant.

Barleria ventricosa
ACANTHACEAE FAMILY
10cm ◇ perennial

Habitat Upland forest and moderate-altitude bushland.
Identification A small, creeping herb with softly hairy, elliptical, dark green leaves. The flowers emerge one by one, but the buds are bunched together at the tips of the stem. The flowers can vary in colour from whitish to pale blue.
Notes This species makes an attractive ground cover.

Crabbea velutina
ACANTHACEAE FAMILY
5cm ◇ perennial

Habitat Dry bush and open grassland, generally in pockets of shallow soil.
Identification This small herb bears its leaves in a basal rosette. They are broadly ovate, stalked and softly hairy, with stiffer hairs along the wavy margins **(1)**. The flowers have five white petals, a pale yellow throat and emerge from leafy bracts with spines along their margins.

Dyschoriste hildebrandtii

ACANTHACEAE FAMILY

20cm ◇ perennial

Habitat Semi-arid bush and *Acacia-Commiphora* woodland; tends to favour rocky slopes.

Identification An upright herb covered with sticky glandular hairs. The leaves are ovate and small (up to 3cm long). The flowers have a long floral tube **(1)** and may vary in colour from white to pale purple. The seed is a woody capsule.

Notes This plant releases a distinctive smell that deters browsing insects, although humans find it pleasing.

Justicia calyculata

ACANTHACEAE FAMILY

15cm ◇ annual/perennial

Habitat Widespread in grassland, from low to moderate altitude; favours shaded positions.

Identification The entire plant is adorned with soft hairs up to 0.1cm long. The leaves are elliptical and the flowers are small, with one upper and three lower lobes.

Notes This plant's small size belies its importance as a food source for bees; it flowers when no other plants are blooming.

Justicia schimperiana
ACANTHACEAE FAMILY
1m ◇ perennial

Habitat Dry, rocky areas and bushland.
Identification A large *Justicia* with hairy stems. The leaves are ovate to elliptical, with slightly wavy margins. They have a shiny green upper surface and a duller undersurface. The attractive flowers are nearly stalkless, peeping out of large, white-edged bracts **(1)**. The sepals have stalked glands. Seeds are borne in a woody capsule.

Thunbergia guerkeana
ACANTHACEAE FAMILY
3m ◇ perennial

Habitat Confined to dry, low-altitude *Acacia-Commiphora* woodland.
Identification A robust climber with broadly ovate, dark green leaves that have a pointed tip and entire, slightly inward-curling edges. The flowers are attractive, with a floral tube up to 10cm long, and strongly recurved petals **(1)**. The sepals are thin and the calyx has a white interior. When dry, the large woody capsule **(2)** containing the seeds splits open to release them.
Notes The flowers are probably pollinated by hawk moths at night.

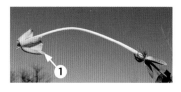

Delosperma nakurense

AIZOACEAE FAMILY
12cm ◇ perennial

Habitat Generally uncommon and found only in rocky situations.
Identification This low-lying herb is usually found among thick bush and is hard to detect, except when in flower. It is succulent with narrow leaves up to 5cm long. The flowers are carried on hairless stalks, and are about 2cm across, with many fine, white petals. When rain falls, the dry capsules open, releasing their seeds.

Aerva javanica

AMARANTHACEAE FAMILY
1m ◇ perennial

Habitat Exclusive to dry *Acacia-Commiphora* woodland and open semi-desert areas.
Identification A tall, upright herb with long, lanceolate, greyish-green leaves. The inflorescence is a panicle with many small, fluffy white flowers along each stem. The sepals are 0.2–0.3cm long. When flowering, the plant has a woolly appearance.
Notes The fluffy inflorescences were once used to stuff mattresses and pillows. This is an attractive plant for gardens in arid areas.

Crinum macowanii
AMARYLLIDACEAE FAMILY
40cm ◇ perennial

Habitat Upland *Acacia-Commiphora* bushland; also occurs close to rivers, seasonal streams and springs.
Identification This lily arises from a large underground bulb, producing a rosette of strappy grey-green leaves just after the first rains. Bunches of up to 12 large, bell-shaped white flowers, with narrow pink stripes on the undersides, hang from a single 30cm-long stem.
Notes The flowers are pollinated by hawk moths at night.

Crinum stuhlmannii
AMARYLLIDACEAE FAMILY
20cm ◇ perennial

Habitat Coastal belt bushland; often occurs near seasonal pans.
Identification Like *C. macowanii*, this *Crinum* arises from an underground bulb and produces a rosette of leaves, but these are paler green and glossier. A thick stem arises from the middle of the rosette, bearing up to six flowers, which are more upright and have larger petals than those of *C. macowanii*. The petals are white, with a broad pink stripe running down the middle of each. The fruit are up to 7cm wide and are pinkish red.

Sericocomopsis hildebrandtii
AMARANTHACEAE FAMILY
1m ◇ perennial

Habitat Fairly common in semi-arid bushland and in degraded habitat at lower altitude.
Identification A multi-branched herb with hairy stems and a greyish overall appearance, *S. hildebrandtii* often scrambles into a shrub if given the chance and may then exceed its average size. The leaves are obovate and softly hairy. Small flowers are borne on a raceme 10–15cm long. Soft white hairs cover the sepals, giving the flowers a woolly look.
Notes This is an important source of fodder for livestock, especially during dry periods when grass is not available.

Pancratium tenuifolium
AMARYLLIDACEAE FAMILY
20cm ◇ annual

Habitat Dry bushland following the rains; may also cover large areas in seasonally waterlogged pans that are drying out.
Identification A small lily that occurs in groups. The leaves, which are a dark shiny green, emerge from the base and lie just above the surface of the ground. The flowering stems are pale yellow and carry delicate white flowers with strap-shaped lobes (1).

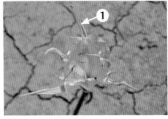

Chlorophytum cameronii var. *pterocaulon*
ANTHERICACEAE FAMILY
25cm ◇ perennial

Habitat Highland grassland and rocky slopes with shallow granitic soils. Usually appears in open, sunny situations after the first rains.
Identification This plant grows from a tuber and has a fibrous root system. It is upright with long, smooth, hairless leaves that have distinctive spotted bases **(1)**. The flowering stalk is somewhat flattened and bears clusters of delicate white flowers.

Chlorophytum cameronii var. *cameronii*
ANTHERICACEAE FAMILY
10cm ◇ perennial

Habitat Favours black cotton soils in open grassland at about 1,500m.
Identification An upright plant with spreading leaves that emerge from the base. The leaves are hairless except for the slightly hairy margins. Stalkless white flowers are closely arranged along the stem.

Chlorophytum gallabatense
ANTHERICACEAE FAMILY
25cm ◇ annual

Habitat Widespread in shallow soils, at altitudes of between 750 and 2,100m. Common after the first rains.
Identification A small lily that grows from a compact root system. Leaves emerge from the base; they are soft, with wavy margins and obvious dark stripes on the underside. The flowers are small, with petals that bend slightly backward, and are white with greenish central markings. The seeds are winged.

Chlorophytum macrophyllum
ANTHERICACEAE FAMILY
16cm ◇ perennial

Habitat Open grassland and bushland; seems to favour black cotton soils.
Identification This lily has many shiny green leaves, each up to 25cm long and 5cm wide. Three to five flowering stalks emerge from the base, bearing flowers about 3cm across. Black seeds are borne in a winged fruit capsule.

Chlorophytum sylvaticum
ANTHERICACEAE FAMILY
12cm ◇ annual

Habitat Open grassland and
woodland at higher altitudes.
Identification A small, upright lily
with fleshy roots. It bears strap-like
leaves from a central rosette at the
base of the plant. They turn slightly
inwards and measure up to 10cm in
length. Small white flowers (up to
0.5cm) are carried close to the stalk,
forming a cylindrical flowering head
about 8–10cm long.

Cynanchum gerrardii
APOCYNACEAE FAMILY
3m ◇ perennial

Habitat Thickets in dry bushland.
Identification This fairly well-
camouflaged climber is leafless and
has succulent stems that are purplish
with faint white lines. The flowers are
borne in small clusters at intervals
along the stem. They are very small,
with backward-curving white petals.
Notes The young stems are edible
and have a tart taste.

Gomphocarpus physocarpus
APOCYNACEAE FAMILY
2m ◇ perennial

Habitat Widespread in open grassland that is prone to flooding, and along roadsides.
Identification A tall plant with leafy stems. The leaves are lanceolate and broadest in the middle. Umbels of creamy white flowers spring from a common centre. The fruits **(1)** are hairy and swollen, containing fluffy seeds.
Notes This attractive plant draws a range of insects to the garden.

Kanahia laniflora
APOCYNACEAE FAMILY
2m ◇ perennial

Habitat Along rivers or streams in otherwise dry regions, and sometimes on islands in a river.
Identification A smooth herb that thrives where its roots are in or near water. Many branches arise from a central point. The leaves are narrow and linear. Large creamy white flowers (up to 3cm across) are borne in bunches at the tops of stems. The petal margins are hairy **(1)**. The fruiting pod is up to 5cm long.

Pergularia daemia
APOCYNACEAE FAMILY
3m ◇ perennial

Habitat Widespread in dry habitats at moderate altitude; also along the margins of cedar-olive forest.
Identification This is a widespread climber with strong stems that are covered in short hairs. The leaves are up to 5cm long, heart-shaped and deeply notched at the base. The flowers, borne in bunches, have greenish or purplish petals with eye-catching white centres. The seed pods **(1)** are narrow and covered in hair-like structures; they burst when ripe, releasing fluffy seeds **(2)**.

Saba comorensis
APOCYNACEAE FAMILY
10m ◇ perennial

Habitat In coastal belt vegetation and close to springs and lakes in dry habitats.
Identification This rather tenacious climber has a dark reddish stem adorned with small, raised, white stripes (lenticels). The leaves are leathery, up to 6cm long, with a glossy upper surface. Flowers smell similar to those of *Carissa* or *Jasminum* species and are borne in bunches, with white petals that curl slightly backwards. The fruit is similar in size to an orange.
Notes The pulp surrounding the seeds is edible when ripe, and is much loved by primates.

Asparagus africanus
ASPARAGACEAE FAMILY
2m ◇ **perennial**

Habitat Often found along forest margins in upland habitat or in thickets in drier areas; fairly abundant where it occurs.

Identification A rather woody plant that grows from a fibrous rootstock. Older stems are smooth and brown with brown spines, each with a spur. The needle-like leaves (cladodes) hang down in bunches. Bears small white flowers and red berries.

Notes Young stems are eaten by humans.

Asparagus falcatus
ASPARAGACEAE FAMILY
3.5m ◇ **perennial**

Habitat Mainly dry bushland. Also in upland forest at moderate altitude.

Identification A climber with spiny, greyish stems. The leaves (cladodes) are flat and straight or scythe-shaped with a single vein. It produces sprays of fragrant white blossoms. The fruits are bright red when ripe.

Notes This asparagus has attractive, bronze-skinned tubers (1) that are edible when peeled. Although watery and rather bland, they may be a lifesaver in the absence of water. When the roots are exposed, porcupines are often the first to find and eat them.

Trachyandra saltii
ASPHODELACEAE FAMILY
10cm ◇ perennial

Habitat Various, but favours shallow
soils in open grassland.
Identification The leaves emerge
from the base and are linear and
hairy. Many flowers are arranged
along a spike carried on an upright
flowering stalk. The white petals have
a distinctive brown central stripe.
Notes This lily is often the first to
appear at the start of the rains.

Anthemis tigreensis
ASTERACEAE FAMILY
7cm ◇ annual/perennial

Habitat At high altitude along
streams, paths and roadsides and
among moorland grasses.
Identification A small herb with
spreading branches and pinnate
leaves. The flowers have striking
yellow centres.

Echinops hispidus
ASTERACEAE FAMILY
1m ◇ **perennial**

Habitat Locally common in upland forest and grassland.
Identification A robust and upright herb. The leaves are stalked and pinnately lobed, with narrow segments. It bears large (6–9cm), rounded flower heads of white or very pale blue flowerets.

Echinops hoehnelii
ASTERACEAE FAMILY
1m ◇ **perennial**

Habitat At altitudes of 2,000–3,500m, on the margins of forest glades and higher up in the moorland.
Identification An upright herb. The spiky leaves have lobes ending in spines **(1)**. The small, tubular, white flowers are crowded in a rounded head up to 3cm in diameter. The shiny petals bend backwards. The stamens are purple-blue.

Erigeron karvinskianus
ASTERACEAE FAMILY
12cm ◇ perennial

Habitat Varied; this is a widespread, commonly encountered exotic.
Identification Probably originating in North America, this small daisy can spread to cover a wide area. It has narrow leaves, which may be lobed or entire. The flower heads measure about 1cm across and vary in colour from white to pink.

Felicia abyssinica
ASTERACEAE FAMILY
10cm ◇ perennial

Habitat Widespread in various habitats, including open, sandy soil and grassland from low to moderate altitude.
Identification A small, upright herb that often forms pure stands. It has many small, narrow, linear leaves about 3cm long and 0.4cm wide. The flowering stems are 6–8cm long and each carries a solitary flower.

Helichrysum brownei
ASTERACEAE FAMILY
60cm ◇ perennial

Habitat Common at high altitude in heathland on the drier slopes of mountains such as the Aberdares, Mt Kenya and Mt Meru.
Identification A short, bushy herb or shrub with very narrow leaves arranged alternately along the stem. The leaves are greyish with short, soft hairs and taper to a hairless point. This plant bears many bunches of creamy white to pale yellow blooms and is striking when in flower.

Helichrysum glumaceum
ASTERACEAE FAMILY
15cm ◇ perennial

Habitat Open areas in semi-arid grassland and *Acacia* bushland.
Identification A small herb with long, linear, greyish leaves that taper to a point. Small, tubular, white or pale yellow flowers (about 0.4cm long) cluster at the tops of the stems.
Notes When crushed, the plant gives off a slight aroma, reminiscent of mountain flora.

Impatiens tinctoria
BALSAMINACEAE FAMILY
3m ◇ perennial

Habitat Close to streams and waterfalls in highland forest.
Identification A tall, upright, hairless plant that forms large clumps. The leaves are alternately arranged along the stem and are broadly ovate with slightly serrated margins. The white flowers appear in loose bunches at the tops of the stems. There are splashes of purple on the lower petals, which are much larger than the upper ones.

Begonia meyeri-johannis
BEGONIACEAE FAMILY
50cm ◇ perennial

Habitat Wet highland forest.
Identification A climber with smooth, shiny, asymmetrical leaves that taper to a point. The stems are marked with small white flecks. Small groups of white flowers up to 3cm across are arranged on pinkish stems.

Begonia wakefieldii
BEGONIACEAE FAMILY
10cm ◇ perennial

Habitat Damp coastal forest.
Identification A fleshy herb with rounded, slightly asymmetrical, pale green leaves. Bears white to pale pinkish flowers and winged fruits.
Notes This species makes an appealing pot plant, as its leaves have an attractive sheen. It is of conservation concern, as its coastal belt habitat is threatened.

Heliotropium longiflorum
BORAGINACEAE FAMILY
10cm ◇ annual/perennial

Habitat Hot, semi-arid areas; often grows in sand along seasonal gullies (*luggas*).
Identification This rather delicate herb is hairless, with lanceolate leaves up to 10cm long. The white flowers have slightly pointed petals (**1**) and are crowded alternately along a curved stem.

Heliotropium steudnerii subsp. *bullatum*
BORAGINACEAE FAMILY
15cm ◇ perennial

Habitat Widespread at moderate to low altitude.
Identification This variable, hairy herb grows from a well-established rootstock. The lanceolate leaves narrow towards the tip and have obviously indented veins. The flowers are borne in curling cymes that give rise to the nickname 'lambs' tails'. They are small, with rounded white petals and a greenish-yellow throat. The sepals are pointed and hairy.

Cadaba farinosa
CAPPARACEAE FAMILY
7m ◇ perennial

Habitat Dry *Acacia* bushland and open grassland at moderate altitude; also found at low altitude in semi-desert areas.
Identification A conspicuous rounded shrub with many thin, tough branches. The leaves are elliptical and covered in scales, giving them a whitish, powdery appearance (*farinosa* means 'mealy'). The outer sepals are greenish, with white to pinkish petals **(1)** and long green stamens. The seed pod measures about 4–5cm and, when its outer covering peels back, it reveals seeds covered with a bright orange membrane.
Notes The flowers are frequented by butterflies.

Maerua decumbens
CAPPARACEAE FAMILY
1m ◇ perennial

Habitat Bushland or grassland; favours semi-arid and near-desert conditions and sandy soils.
Identification A straggly shrub with many long, thin branches growing from the base. The leaves are circular. Flowers up to 4cm across are carried on a long stem. Petals are absent, but many white stamens spread out from the leafy green calyx. The fruit is a drupe that turns red as it ripens.
Notes Ants and bees take nectar from the base of the stamens.

Sambucus ebulus (S. africana)
CAPRIFOLIACEAE FAMILY
3m ◇ perennial

Habitat This plant is associated with the bamboo zone (found above the montane forest zone).
Identification A tall shrub or herb with soft, upright stems that are very brittle – when elephants pass by, they leave a trail of broken plants. The leaves are large and pinnate, with pointed teeth along the margins. Many small flowers are arranged together in an umbel. The fruits turn black as they ripen.

Pollichia campestris
CARYOPHYLLACEAE FAMILY
20cm ◇ perennial

Habitat Widespread on roadsides, forest edges and in rocky, arid areas.
Identification A small, straggly herb or shrub with narrow, bluish-green leaves carried in whorls at the nodes. They have tiny hairs along their margins. The flowers are generally overlooked, as they are very tiny. The edible raspberry-like fruits, borne in clusters, are often mistaken for flowers. They turn red as they ripen.

Cleome gynandra
(Gynandropsis gynandra)
CLEOMACEAE FAMILY
20cm ◇ perennial

Habitat Abandoned kraals or disturbed ground. Also in dry, open bushland.
Identification This sticky herb may form pure stands. It has palmate leaves and its flowers, which are borne in columns, have up to four loose petals. The stamens and stigma are well exserted and accessible to pollinators, particularly hawk moths.
Notes Young leaves, which emerge at the start of the rains, can be prepared and eaten like spinach.

Androcymbium striatum (*A. melanthoides*)

COLCHICACEAE FAMILY

12cm ◇ **perennial**

Habitat Generally at higher altitude in rocky areas and on black cotton soils.
Identification A small, delicate lily with an underground bulb. The leaves are long, upright and shiny green. The attractive white, green-striped flowers are large, with broad petals.

Astripomoea hyoscyamoides

CONVOLVULACEAE FAMILY

2m ◇ **perennial**

Habitat At lower altitude in dry bushland, where it often forms pure stands; also in areas of cultivation.
Identification A many-branched, shrub-like herb, whose leaves are broad, tapering at the tip, with prominent veins, a softly hairy underside and shallow, widely spaced teeth along the margins. The flowers (5cm across) are white with a purple throat and are crowded at the tops of the stems. The seed pods (1) have a hairy surface.

Ipomoea garckeana
CONVOLVULACEAE FAMILY
3m ◇ perennial

Habitat Among shoreline bush and in coastal forests.
Identification A creeper with long, softly hairy stems and glandular, unusually shaped leaves with three distinct lobes, the upper lobe having a central notch **(1)**. The flowers are rounded, about 7cm across, with a deep purple centre.

Ipomoea hildebrandtii
subsp. *megaensis*
CONVOLVULACEAE FAMILY
2m ◇ perennial

Habitat Bare ground; often grows along roadsides.
Identification A woody herb with multiple branches arising from its base. The leaves are large and rounded, with fine hairs on the undersurface. The flowers and leaves are much larger than those of subsp. *hildebrandtii*. The flowers are often whitish or pale pink, with a purple centre and silky sepals.
Notes Bees collect the pollen.

Ipomoea longituba
CONVOLVULACEAE FAMILY
50cm ◇ **perennial**

Habitat Open plains with mixed lateritic soils; sometimes found in black cotton soils.
Identification This rather robust *Ipomoea* species arises from a large tuber that resembles a sweet potato. The leaves, which are up to 10cm long, are broadly ovate, turn slightly inward and have heavy venation on the undersurface. The flowers are long and tubular, and the petals are papery with a strong midrib. The sepals clasp the floral tube.
Notes This species is pollinated by hawk moths at night. The roots are edible and can be eaten raw.

Ipomoea mombassana
CONVOLVULACEAE FAMILY
1m ◇ **perennial**

Habitat A lowland *Ipomoea* found in grassland, along roadsides and in dry bushland.
Identification A climber with hairy stems and leaves. The leaves are oblong with a heart-shaped base. The white flowers have a purple centre and linear sepals.
Notes This plant is eaten by elephants and is a favourite of stingless bees, which collect the pollen.

Crassula alba
CRASSULACEAE FAMILY
20cm ◇ perennial

Habitat Fairly widespread in dry, rocky bushland or grassland.
Identification A small succulent herb with a basal rosette of lanceolate leaves and some leaves along the stem. Small flowers are carried in bunches in the leaf axils (1) along the flowering stem.

Crassula volkensii subsp. *volkensii*
CRASSULACEAE FAMILY
4cm ◇ perennial

Habitat Rocky semi-arid bushland, usually in a shaded position.
Identification A low-lying herb with small, succulent, purple-tinged leaves. The flowers, too, are small – just 0.5cm across – with entire margins.

Dipsacus pinnatifidus
DIPSACEAE FAMILY
2m ◇ perennial

Habitat Fairly common at high altitude in forest glades and along streams in open grassland.
Identification A tall plant with toothed, ovate leaves arranged in whorls at the nodes on the stems. The stems are covered in stiff glandular hairs **(1)**. Flowers, borne at the tops of the stems in rounded heads, are up to 4cm across.

Sansevieria frequens
DRACAENACEAE FAMILY
1m ◇ perennial

Habitat Widespread in dry, rocky bushland at moderate altitude.
Identification A broad-leafed plant with underground stems (rhizomes). The leaves are upright and green, with red-tinged margins. The inflorescence may be up to a metre tall, emerging from the centre of the leaves. Delicate white to pinkish flowers are crowded along the flowering stems. The fruits turn orange as they ripen.

Notes Weaver birds tear strips from the leaves, which they use for nest-building. This plant flowers at night, emitting a scent that attracts hawk moth pollinators.

Sansevieria robusta
DRACAENACEAE FAMILY
1m ◇ perennial

Habitat Widespread in semi-arid and arid bushland at moderate altitude.
Identification Tall and upright, with leaves that fan out from a thick stem. The leaves are pale green, ribbed, and taper to a sharp spike. Reddish markings are evident where the leaves clasp the stem. A multi-branched inflorescence bears white to pinkish flowers that emit a scent at night. The fruits turn orange when ripe. As this plant can reproduce from rhizomes, it doesn't need to flower every year.
Notes Some traditional communities use the fibre for house-building. Elephants chew the leaves for their juice and spit out the fibres. In degraded soils this plant forms pure stands, providing protection for young succulents and facilitating the germination of seeds.

Pelargonium multibracteatum (*P. alchemilliodes*)
GERANIACEAE FAMILY
40cm ◇ perennial

Habitat Dry bushland, usually within the shelter of a shrub or spiny *Euphorbia*.
Identification A delicate herb belonging to the geranium family. The leaves comprise up to seven lobes, with toothed margins and appressed hairs on the upper surface. Each lobe has attractive purple markings. Up to seven flowers are loosely arranged in an umbel. The sepals are softly hairy.

Pelargonium quinquelobatum

GERANIACEAE FAMILY

15cm ◇ perennial

Habitat In grassland and on rocky ground at moderate to high altitude.
Identification Much more delicate than *P. multibracteatum*, this smallish herb has a tuberous rootstock. The leaves are at the base of the plant and are deeply divided into as many as seven lobes. The flowers vary from white to greenish-yellow.

Albuca donaldsonii (Ornithogalum donaldsonii)

HYACINTHACEAE FAMILY

1m ◇ perennial

Habitat Widespread; found at moderate altitude in dry *Acacia-Commiphora* bushland and in open grassland.
Identification A tall plant that arises from a large bulb. Its has long, shiny green leaves. Large white-petalled flowers with an obvious green midrib are arranged along a tall flowering raceme.
Notes Caterpillars enjoy feeding on the leaves.

Drimia altissima
HYACINTHACEAE FAMILY
1m ◇ perennial

Habitat Very widespread in semi-arid areas at low to moderate altitude; also on the margins of upland forest.
Identification This plant grows from an above-ground bulb up to 12cm in width. The flowers appear before the leaves and have backward-curling petals. They are crowded together along the flowering stem. The leaves are long and tend to bend at the tips.

Ornithogalum tenuifolium
HYACINTHACEAE FAMILY
30cm ◇ perennial

Habitat Widespread in bushland and around seasonal water in grassland habitat.
Identification This plant arises from a round bulb, producing leaves up to 20cm long and about 3cm in width. They are smooth and hairless and curl inward. Many flowers and buds are arranged on a cylindrical raceme. The petals are white with a broad green midrib.

Gladiolus candidus
IRIDACEAE FAMILY
35cm ◇ perennial

Habitat Occurs around seasonal water, in damp, rocky areas, and on black cotton soils.
Identification This iris comes up after good rains. Long leaves with a central ridge appear at the same time as the flowering stalk. The flowers have six crisp white petals, each marked with a prominent midrib and tapering from a broad base to a narrow, pointed tip.

Gladiolus pauciflorus
IRIDACEAE FAMILY
50cm ◇ annual

Habitat Dry grassland.
Identification This seldom encountered, tall, upright lily has flat, grass-like leaves, making it hard to spot among grasses when not in flower. The blooms are creamy white, with a dash of deep red at the base of the petals. The floral tube is equal in length to the petals.

Fuerstia africana

LAMIACEAE FAMILY
30cm ◇ perennial

Habitat This herb is widespread on forest margins in upland areas and in dry bushland at moderate altitude.
Identification A delicate herb with squarish, upright stems. The leaves are broadly elliptical and softly hairy. Small, two-lipped flowers are loosely arranged at the tops of the stems. Both leaves and flowers are covered with reddish glands.
Notes This plant is known as 'ochre of the rhino' in Maa. When crushed, it produces a bright red 'staining' juice **(1)** that, in the absence of ochre, young Maasai girls traditionally use to decorate their faces. Bees take nectar from the flowers.

Leucas glabrata

LAMIACEAE FAMILY
3m ◇ annual/perennial

Habitat Common in a variety of habitats, from semi-arid bushland to forest margins.
Identification A softly hairy herb or shrub with squarish stems and stalked, elliptical to ovate leaves with toothed margins. Two-lipped flowers appear in clusters at well-spaced intervals along the stem. The upper petal is softly hairy and the lower petal has three lobes.
Notes The flowers are a favourite with carpenter bees, which visit them regularly.

Leucas grandis
LAMIACEAE FAMILY
2m ◇ **perennial**

Habitat Found at moderate altitude in *Carissa* and *Rhus* bushland and, less commonly, in dry *Acacia-Commiphora* bushland.

Identification A tall, more robust plant than *L. glabrata*, with hairs along the stems. The leaves are about 8cm long, broad, tapering towards the apex and have toothed margins. The white flowers are borne in rounded heads at the nodes. The upper lip **(1)** of the flower is hairy and about 2cm long.

Ocimum americanum
LAMIACEAE FAMILY
50cm ◇ **annual/perennial**

Habitat Dry bushland. Also occurs along ditches and roads.

Identification An upright herb with tough, squarish, hairy stems. The leaves are rounded or elliptical and softly hairy. They give off a lemon-like smell when crushed. Pale, two-lipped flowers are carried on a long inflorescence.

Notes This plant is an important source of nectar for bees, and is used by some local communities to encourage bees to occupy a new beehive. This is done by rubbing the plant inside the prospective hive and leaving some stems and leaves at its entrance. The leaves can also be used to brew a herbal tea.

Ocimum gratissimum
LAMIACEAE FAMILY
1m ◇ perennial

Habitat Forest margins and open glades at moderate to high altitude. It also occurs among hedges separating cultivated plots.
Identification This shrubby *Ocimum* has lanceolate leaves, each about 4cm long, with toothed margins. They are variegated in green and greenish-yellow and are aromatic when crushed. The flowers are small and two-lipped.
Notes This plant is valued for its medicinal properties. The leaves can be chewed to numb stomach pains.

Ocimum kenyense
LAMIACEAE FAMILY
20cm ◇ perennial

Habitat Damp situations in black cotton soils at about 1,500–1,800m.
Identification This plant has squarish stems and smooth, ovate leaves with entire or serrate margins. The leaves become purplish as they dry out. Flowers are borne on an inflorescence covered in short, soft hairs. All parts of the plant emit a distincitve smell when crushed, a scent often detected on walks or drives through areas with black cotton soils.
Notes The perfumed leaves are threaded among the beads worn for traditional ceremonies by some local communities.

Ocimum kilimandscharicum
LAMIACEAE FAMILY
1m ◇ perennial

Habitat On the margins of dry cedar-olive forests at altitudes above 6,800m.
Identification A robust, softly hairy herb or shrub with conspicuous, squarish, purple stems. The leaves are opposite, elliptical and broad at the base, narrowing towards the tip. White flowers with purple bracts are arranged along a 20cm-long raceme. The entire plant is aromatic, particularly the leaves.

Notes Essential oil can be extracted from the leaves for use in soaps and cosmetics. This plant is also an important source of nectar for bees.

Ocimum obovatum
LAMIACEAE FAMILY
20cm ◇ perennial

Habitat Open grassland at higher altitude.
Identification An upright herb with small white hairs on the stems, and variable, ovate, toothed leaves, which measure up to 4cm in length and are softly hairy. White flowers are arranged in whorls at the tips of the branches; the inner petals have purple striping.

Hibiscus cannabinus
MALVACEAE FAMILY
2.5m ◇ perennial

Habitat Favours wet situations and black cotton soils, as well as roadside ditches containing stagnant water.
Identification A tall, shrubby herb with two or three stems arising from the base. The leaves are palmate and rounded, with deep lobes. The leaflets are narrow, with toothed margins. The shape of the leaf resembles that of *Cannabis sativa*, hence the name. The white flowers are 10–12cm across and have a purple centre that can vary in intensity depending on the minerals in the soil. The seed pods are covered in hairs.

Hibiscus flavifolius
MALVACEAE FAMILY
2m ◇ perennial

Habitat Open grassland, often in areas overgrazed by livestock.
Identification A tall, woody, upright plant with just a few branches arising from the main stem, and broadly ovate leaves covered in star-shaped golden hairs. The flowers are solitary and emerge from the leaf axils. There are bright orange pollinia at the centre of the anthers.

Hibiscus fuscus
MALVACEAE FAMILY
2m ◇ perennial

Habitat Widespread; sizeable pure stands are found on open ground or in grassland.
Identification A tall, upright perennial with obvious long, dark hairs on the stems. The leaves are ovate, narrowing towards the tip, with toothed margins

and a covering of soft hairs. The five-petalled flowers open fully during the day and close in the afternoon. The sepals are pointed and clothed in dark hairs.

Nymphaea lotus
NYMPHAEACEAE FAMILY
2m ◇ perennial

Habitat Found mainly at Lake Victoria but also in some seasonal pools along the coastal belt. It is less common than other *Nymphaea* species.
Identification The leaves of this water lily are rounded, large and entire, with a shiny upper surface. The flowers are large – up to 20cm in diameter.

Jasminum fluminense
OLEACEAE FAMILY
3m ◇ perennial

Habitat Varies, from low-lying, arid bushland to forest margins at moderate altitude.

Identification All parts of this tough climber, but especially the leaves, are obviously hairy, although this is less pronounced in plants growing at higher altitude. The leaves are compound, consisting of 3–5 ovate leaflets. Hairy domatia are evident at the base of the leaflets on their undersurface. The flowers are borne in bunches and have a white or pinkish floral tube. As they ripen, the berries turn black.

Aerangis brachycarpa
ORCHIDACEAE FAMILY
10cm ◇ perennial

Habitat Upland forest and dry cedar-olive forests, where it is usually found growing on low, mossy branches.

Identification This perennial epiphyte has short, woody stems with thick, ovate, dark green leaves that are narrower at the base and broadest at the tip. Attractive, star-like flowers hang down in a long spike and turn white as they mature. The tail-like spur **(1)** behind the flower is long and thin, measuring up to 15cm, and both the sepals and the petals bend backward.

Aerangis confusa
ORCHIDACEAE FAMILY
12cm ◇ perennial

Habitat Low, mossy tree branches in upland forest.
Identification This epiphytic orchid is very similar to *A. brachycarpa*. The stems are pendent, and the leaves are in a fan-like arrangement. They are narrow at the base, with a broader, two-lobed tip. Up to 10 flowers are arranged on each long spike, and the petals (but not the sepals) bend backward. The spur is much shorter than that of *A. brachycarpa*, reaching just 4–6cm.

Aerangis luteo-alba
ORCHIDACEAE FAMILY
12cm ◇ perennial

Habitat Trees and shrubs in small woodland forests within the Mara and Serengeti. Favours slightly warmer areas.
Identification A small epiphytic orchid with fairly short stems. The leaves are usually also short, with unequal lobes at the tip. They attain about 10cm in length and 2cm in width. *A. luteo-alba* is one of East Africa's most attractive wild orchids. The showy white flowers have a red centre, and alternate along the stem, facing upward. They have six petals, each ending in a small pointed tip.

Aerangis thomsonii
ORCHIDACEAE FAMILY
20cm ◇ perennial

Habitat Widespread in dry upland forests and in relict vegetation near rivers and streams. Found hanging from trees, cliffs or rocks.
Identification A robust orchid, often found growing in large bunches. It has a tough root system and a woody stem over 10cm long. The leaves are thick, with an indent at the tip. Attractive sprays of flowers make this plant conspicuous in tall trees or on rock faces. The petals bend backward.

Angraecum eburneum
subsp. *giryamae*
ORCHIDACEAE FAMILY
1m ◇ perennial

Habitat This epiphytic species is confined to the coastal belt and to certain offshore islands, such as Pemba. May be found growing on old fossilised coral outcrops or, sometimes, in trees.
Identification A tough-looking plant with thick, woody stems from which hang many roots. The leaves are wide, up to 70cm long, with slightly serrated margins. The inflorescences emerge from leafless areas on the thick stem. The flowers are large (up to 8cm including the spur) and scented, with greenish-white sepals.

Angraecum erectum
ORCHIDACEAE FAMILY
1m ◇ perennial

Habitat This epiphytic species is widespread in dry areas at low altitude. It may grow on the ground or climb up onto rocks or into bushes.
Identification The stems are straight and upright, attaining 1m or more. The leaves are fairly stiff and leathery, with uneven pointed lobes at their tips. The flowers emerge, one at a time, from the leaf axils.

Bonatea steudneri
ORCHIDACEAE FAMILY
1m ◇ perennial

Habitat In dry bushland at moderate altitude, mostly in rocky situations or under the protection of a shrub or *Acacia*.
Identification An upright orchid that grows from an underground bulb. Most of the leaves spread out at the base, but some clasp the flowering stem. The inflorescence consists of whitish-green flowers with long (up to 20cm), twisted spurs.

Rangaeris amaniensis
ORCHIDACEAE FAMILY
2m ◇ perennial

Habitat Dry cedar-olive forests, where it grows epiphytically.
Identification This species has long, branched stems and thick greyish roots. It bears tough leaves with a slight notch at the tip. Up to 12 flowers, white but fading to yellowish, each with six petals and a long spur **(1)**, are borne in a tight raceme. One of the petals forms a lanceolate lower lip **(2)**.

Vanilla roscherii
ORCHIDACEAE FAMILY
10m ◇ perennial

Habitat Commonly known as the vanilla orchid, this plant occurs along the coastal belt and in thick bush extending inland for some 30–40km.
Identification A climber with smooth, succulent stems up to 2cm in diameter, and scales rather than leaves. The white flowers, which are quite large (up to 6cm across), make for a dramatic sight in the bush.
Notes The related *V. planifolia* is grown commercially in Madagascar, where the pods are used to produce vanilla essence.

Cycnium tubulosum
OROBANCHACEAE FAMILY
12cm ◇ perennial

Habitat Widespread in many habitats. It favours shallow soil in open grassland and can tolerate the margins of soda lakes.
Identification This creeping herb has a tough rootstock and is semi-parasitic on other plants, particularly grasses. The leaves are toothed and narrow. The flowers range in colour from white to various shades of pink, depending on the mineral content of the soil where it grows.

Adenia volkensii
PASSIFLORACEAE FAMILY
1m ◇ perennial

Habitat Among rocks in dry *Acacia* bushland.
Identification An upright plant with several thick stems arising from an underground taproot. The leaves are rounded in outline, deeply lobed, with reddish veins. There is a stalked gland at the base of each leaf. The flowers are bell-shaped and up to 3cm in length. Green-and-white at first, the fruits **(1)** turn bright red as they ripen.

Peperomia tetraphylla
PIPERACEAE FAMILY
15cm ◇ perennial

Habitat Damp upland forests, where it grows on mossy branches.
Identification This epiphytic herb is smooth and hairless, except for the stem of the flowering spike. It bears whorls of up to four somewhat fleshy, shiny green leaves with a rounded or elliptical shape. The flowers are tiny, and the seeds are small and black.
Notes This attractive wild herb does well in a pot.

Clematis brachiata
RANUNCULACEAE FAMILY
3m ◇ perennial

Habitat Widespread along forest edges and in bushy thickets within grassland.
Identification A climber with tough stems and rounded, compact leaves comprising lobed leaflets. Showy, creamy white flowers are borne in large bunches. The fruiting parts of the flower are clothed in silky hairs.

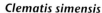

Clematis simensis
RANUNCULACEAE FAMILY
3m ◇ perennial

Habitat Forest margins and upland bushland.
Identification A large, shrubby climber with ovate, entire, not lobed leaves that are somewhat glossy. The sweet-scented flowers are about 2cm across.
Notes The indigenous *Clematis* species of the region are not as showy as those occurring in Europe, but they are still attractive when in flower – and even more so when bearing seeds (1).

Caylusea abyssinica
RESEDACEAE FAMILY
1m ◇ annual/perennial

Habitat Open areas with sparse grass cover or bare ground. Widespread at a variety of altitudes.
Identification A delicate herb that branches from its base. The stems are ridged, covered in glandular hairs and bear lanceolate leaves in bunches. The flowers are arranged along a 20cm-long raceme and have tiny white petals up to 1.2cm long. There are 12–15 pink or orange stamens.

Rubus keniensis
ROSACEAE FAMILY
2m ◇ perennial

Habitat Abundant in montane forests.
Identification This scrambling shrub
is covered in long, soft hairs. Each
compound leaf comprises three leaflets
with toothed margins. The white to
pale pink flowers are bunched in a
loose panicle. Young fruits are green,
turning red as they ripen.
Notes The fruits **(1)** resemble wild
blackberries, but are rather flavourless.

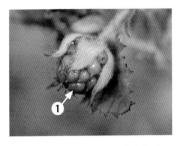

Agathisanthemum bojeri
RUBIACEAE FAMILY
15cm ◇ annual

Habitat Confined to the coast, where
it is found mainly in damp situations.
Identification This annual has upright
stems and lanceolate, opposite leaves,
which are carried on short shoots at
the nodes. Small, bell-shaped flowers
(about 1cm) are borne in heads at the
tips of the branches. The sepals have
green stripes and tiny marginal teeth.

Carphalea glaucescens
RUBIACEAE FAMILY
1.2m ◇ **perennial**

Habitat Sandy soils in dry *Acacia-Commiphora* bushland.
Identification A tall shrub with pale green, lanceolate leaves measuring up to 7cm. Small white flowers with a long floral tube are surrounded by an unusual bright pink calyx **(1)**.
Notes An important source of fodder for goats in semi-arid areas where grass is absent for most of the year.

Conostomium quadrangulare
RUBIACEAE FAMILY
20cm ◇ **annual**

Habitat Rocky situations in dry bushland.
Identification All parts of this upright plant are covered in long hairs, especially the leaves **(1)**, which are opposite, lanceolate and up to 8cm long. They are stalkless and clasp the main stem. Four-petalled, star-shaped flowers are carried on pinkish flowering stalks.

Diodia aulacosperma
RUBIACEAE FAMILY
5cm ◇ annual

Habitat Coastal sand dunes; also in coastal bush extending slightly inland.
Identification A small, creeping herb, with angular stems and succulent, elliptical leaves up to 5cm long.
The flowers are small (about 1cm in diameter), with four pointed petals.

Otomeria oculata
RUBIACEAE FAMILY
15cm ◇ perennial

Habitat Rocky crevices on granitic hills in hot, dry areas.
Identification A many-branched, upright herb with wavy-edged, oval leaves. The flowers have a purplish floral tube, about 1.7cm long. Each of the five white to pinkish petals has a tiny purple spot at its apex.

Paederia prospischilii
RUBIACEAE FAMILY
3m ◇ perennial

Habitat *Acacia-Commiphora* woodland; occasionally also found on rocky escarpments.
Identification An uncommon climber with narrow or rounded, opposite leaves. Striking·white flowers with a pale pink centre emerge in bunches from the leaf axils. Delicate hairs adorn the edges of the petals. The seeds are oval, with a persistent and obvious calyx that is typical in members of the Rubiaceae.

Cardiospermum grandiflorum
SAPINDACEAE FAMILY
10m ◇ perennial

Habitat Along the coastal belt and in *Acacia-Commiphora* bushland at low altitude.
Identification An attractive climber with compound leaves, comprising three leaflets of which the terminal leaflet is largest. The leaf margins are unevenly toothed and slightly hairy. Small, white, yellow-centred flowers with petals 0.3–0.4cm long are borne in bunches. The fruits **(1)** are round and papery.

Craterostigma hirsutum
SCROPHULARIACEAE FAMILY
8cm ◇ annual

Habitat In shallow soil near standing water in rock pools.
Identification A small plant with unbranched, pale yellow, fibrous roots. The leaves are arranged in a basal rosette, are broadly lanceolate, with a warty upper surface and long, sparse white hairs both above and below. The inflorescence is about 8cm tall, with flowers bunched together at its tip. The flowers are white with violet patches on the lower lobes, and yellow stamens.

Hebenstretia angolensis
SCROPHULARIACEAE FAMILY
50cm ◇ perennial

Habitat Montane grassland and open heath; abundant at altitudes from about 3,600m upward. Also found in volcanic soil along the edges of montane lakes and tarns.
Identification This plant is smooth and hairless with narrow linear leaves. Small white flowers, with a solitary upturned white petal emblazoned with a red central stripe, are carried on a 6–10cm-long spike.

Chascanum hildebrandtii
VERBENACEAE FAMILY
50cm ◇ **perennial**

Habitat Shallow soil overlying rock in dry country.
Identification A very pretty little herb with a woody root system. The leaves are elliptical, covered in long hairs and have slightly toothed margins. Small white flowers are carried on a long spike.

Lantana viburnoides
VERBENACEAE FAMILY
3m ◇ **perennial**

Habitat Widespread In *Carissa* or *Rhus* bushland at 1,500–1,800m. It is often found deep within a thicket.
Identification A woody herb or shrub with opposite, ovate leaves. The leaf margins are serrate and rough to the touch. The flowers are generally white (rarely pinkish) with a yellow throat and a white corolla.

Lippia javanica
VERBENACEAE FAMILY
2m ◇ perennial

Habitat On the margins of relict forest
at moderate altitude. It is especially
prolific in deforested areas, where
cedar-olive forest previously occurred.
Identification A shrubby plant with
hairy, purplish stems. The leaves
are lanceolate, with softly toothed
margins. Tiny flowers with a yellow
throat are carried close to the stem
in stalkless rounded heads with hairy
bracts. The seeds are dry.
Notes The fresh leaves can be used to
brew a very pleasant herbal tea.

Lippia kituiensis
VERBENACEAE FAMILY
3m ◇ perennial

Habitat Widespread at moderate to
low altitude.
Identification A bushy shrub. The
plant is less hairy than *L. javanica.*
The leaves are toothed, dark green
and somewhat shiny, broad at the
base and narrower towards the tip.
Rounded heads comprising many
small, yellow-throated flowers are
carried on 4cm-long stems. The
strong fragrance of this plant can be
detected, even when one is driving
through an area where it is flowering.

Priva curtisiae
VERBENACEAE FAMILY
15cm ◇ annual

Habitat Locally common in
dry areas.
Identification An erect, hairy
herb from a woody rootstock. The
leaves are hairy and sllightly sticky,
oblong, up to 5 x 4cm, with toothed
margins. Flowers are white, on a
long, unbranched raceme with sticky
sepals. The fruits are slightly beaked
and hairy.

Cissus quadrangularis
VITACEAE FAMILY
5m ◇ perennial

Habitat Dry bushland and
forest margins.
Identification A fairly widespread
climber with distinctive winged
stems **(1)**. The leaves have three or four
lobes, and the flowers **(2)** are small,
with backward-turned petals. The fruits
are green, turning yellow as they ripen.
Notes A number of bee species
collect nectar from the flowers.

Cissus rotundifolia
VITACEAE FAMILY
8m ◇ perennial

Habitat Dry and *Acacia-Commiphora* bushland at low altitude and *Acacia* bushland at moderate altitude.
Identification A widespread, robust climber that often completely covers trees in drier areas. It has a thick stem (up to 5cm in older plants) and tough tendrils. The leaves are fleshy, rounded, greyish-green, and curve slightly. The flowers can be whitish or yellowish, and the fruits turn red as they ripen.
Notes The small flowers attract bees, flies and wasps. In drier areas elephants also browse on this plant.

Cyphostemma serpens
VITACEAE FAMILY
40cm ◇ perennial

Habitat Widespread at moderate altitude in *Acacia* grassland and at lower altitude on bare, degraded soils.
Identification A compact herb that grows close to the ground. It has hairy, glandular, palmate leaves and small flowers **(1)**. The berries turn bright red when ripe.
Notes The fruits are edible and a good source of vitamin C. Leopard Tortoises enjoy eating the leaves.

Asystasia guttata

ACANTHACEAE FAMILY

30cm ◆ perennial

Habitat Semi-arid and arid *Acacia-Commiphora* bushland and *Acacia* grassland.

Identification This herb arises from a woody rootstock. The leaves have slightly wavy margins and are broadly ovate, narrowing to a pointed tip. The flowering spike is up to 8cm long. Stalkless flowers emerge from pointed, leafy bracts **(1)** that are covered in soft hairs. The inner petals are creamy yellow, flecked with brown spots.

Barleria eranthemoides

ACANTHACEAE FAMILY

40cm ◆ perennial

Habitat Open, semi-arid grassland and *Euphorbia* bushland, usually in full or partial sun.

Identification A small, compact shrub that branches from the base. It has broad, elliptical, dark green leaves and 3–4 sharp, 1cm-long spines in the leaf axils **(1)**. The flowers are carried in spiny flower heads and have five petals. The fruit is a capsule with two valves.

Notes Grevy's Zebras, rhinos and camels all feed on this plant.

Justicia flava
ACANTHACEAE FAMILY
40cm ✤ **perennial**

Habitat Widespread in semi-arid areas, at low to moderate altitude.
Identification A tall, woody herb with 6cm-long ovate leaves that narrow to a point and have a smooth surface and wavy margins. The flowers are carried on a spike, which is covered in thin green bracts less than 0.2cm in width.

Justicia odora
ACANTHACEAE FAMILY
60cm ✤ **perennial**

Habitat Varies from very dry bushland and rocky areas at low altitude to forest margins at moderate altitude.
Identification A widespread, woody herb with angular, hairy or smooth, greyish-white stems. The leaves are broadly elliptical, up to 1cm long, smooth and hairless. The yellow flowers are two-lipped, with the lower lip divided into three lobes.
Notes The bark has a vanilla-like scent. Some communities use it to make traditional scented necklaces and bracelets. Ochre and sheep's fat are used to preserve the perfume.

Thunbergia fischeri
ACANTHACEAE FAMILY
10cm ◆ perennial

Habitat Found in grassland at moderate altitude and in upland forest.
Identification A creeping herb with soft hairs on the leaves and stems. The leaves are nearly stalkless, obovate, with wavy margins. The flowers have five slightly lobed, lemon-yellow petals **(1)**.

Haplosciadium abyssinicum
APIACEAE FAMILY
10cm ◆ perennial

Habitat Open areas in upland grassland. Also occurs close to streams and rivers in dryland riverine vegetation.
Identification This small herb has a prostrate habit. The leaves **(1)** form a rosette and are pinnate, comprising closely arranged leaflets with pointed tips. Flower umbels 3–4cm across are carried on the many thick flowering stems that emerge from the centre of the rosette.

Cynanchum viminale
APOCYNACEAE FAMILY
3m perennial

Habitat Varies from dry *Acacia* bushland and cedar-olive forest to upland forest and forest margins.
Identification A widespread, tenacious and robust climber with fleshy stems and no leaves. The cream to yellow flowers, which are borne in bunches, have forward-folding petals (**1**) up to 0.8cm long. The twin seed pods each measure 6cm.
Notes This plant is a favourite of camels, giraffes and Greater Kudu, and the flowers are an important source of nectar for bees. In addition, the young stems are chewed, and the slightly bitter juice swallowed as a traditional medicine for sore throats.

Gomphocarpus fruticosus
APOCYNACEAE FAMILY
3m perennial

Habitat A tall multi-branching shrub with narrow, lanceolate leaves borne in bunches. The leaves are smooth, with entire margins. Flowers with backward-bending greenish-yellow petals hang in attractive sprays. The inflated fruit (**1**) narrows to a point and is clothed in soft hairs. Inside, the seeds are adorned with soft, silky fibres that aid in wind dispersal.
Notes Monarch butterflies sip the nectar, which is poisonous and renders the insects unpalatable to birds.

Gomphocarpus stenophyllus
APOCYNACEAE FAMILY
2m ⬦ **perennial**

Habitat Generally at moderate altitude along roadsides, in grassland and on patches of bare ground in *Acacia* bushland.
Identification This plant, which has multiple branches arising from the base, bears very narrow leaves and woolly white hairs on all parts. Numerous umbels **(1)** of red-tinged yellow flowers hang like bells from the tops of the flowering stalks. The fruits are smooth and narrow.

Orbea dummeri
(Pachycymbium dummeri)
APOCYNACEAE FAMILY
5cm ⬦ **perennial**

Habitat Rocky hills, dry bushland and *Acacia* woodland.
Identification A succulent herb with slightly variegated, green-and-purplish trailing stems up to 1cm in width. The stems are marked with soft, pointed projections **(1)**. Hairy, star-like, yellowish green flowers are carried at the tips of the branches. Stiff glandular hairs cover the petal lobes.
Notes The young stems are edible and usually chewed to quench a thirst. They are quite bitter!

MWS

Bulbine abyssinica
ASPHODELACEAE FAMILY
20cm   perennial

Habitat Highly variable; favours shallow soils.
Identification This small, upright lily has a tuberous root system and emerges after good rains. The leaves are thin and fleshy, up to 35cm long and 0.5–0.8cm wide. Flowers (about 2cm across) with green midrib and six petals, borne on a tall flowering stem **(1)**. The seeds are black.

Acmella caulirhiza
ASTERACEAE FAMILY
20cm   annual

Habitat Upland grassland, where it is common. In drier areas it favours wet situations along rivers or near to permanent springs.
Identification A trailing herb with small (up to 3cm), oval, dark green leaves that have toothed margins. The flowering heads are compact and bright, with very small yellow to orange petals **(1)**.
Notes The flowers have a numbing effect when chewed and can be used to alleviate toothache.

Aspilia mossambicensis
ASTERACEAE FAMILY
1m ◆ perennial

Habitat Widespread in dry bushland and open *Acacia* grassland at moderate altitude.
Identification A woody herb that may grow into a shrub if supported by surrounding vegetation. The leaves are up to 6cm long, elliptical, rough and hairy; the flowers are about 3cm across and creamy yellow to orange.
Notes In traditional medicine the leaves are crushed to a pulp and applied directly to a cut or wound to staunch bleeding.

Berkheya spekeana
ASTERACEAE FAMILY
1m ◆ perennial

Habitat Upland grassland and forest margins.
Identification An upright, prickly herb. The leaves clasp the stems, are divided into pinnate lobes and have short marginal spines. The flower heads are up to 5cm wide, and the petals are long with a notch at the tip.
Notes The Pokot roast the leaves and apply the ash as a treatment for wounds.

Bidens kilimandscharica
ASTERACEAE FAMILY
2m perennial

Habitat Found mostly in
montane heathland.
Identification All parts of this short-
lived shrub are hairy. The leaves are
pinnate, with toothed lobes, and the
flowers are very showy, emerging in
large bunches at the top of the plant.
The yellow flowers measure up to
3cm across.

Bidens ugandensis
ASTERACEAE FAMILY
50cm perennial

Habitat At moderate altitude in shallow
soil overlying rock, and in dry bushland.
Identification A very delicate plant
with straggly stems. The leaves (1) are
thinly pinnate, smooth and hairless.
The flowers are golden yellow and
measure up to 3cm across.

Cineraria deltoidea
ASTERACEAE FAMILY
80cm ❀ **perennial**

Habitat Forest margins and rocky cliffs.
Identification A tall herb with loose
branches and triangular, toothed
leaves (**1**). It bears a profusion of
flowers each up to 1cm across. All
parts of the plant are hairy.

Dendrosenecio keniensis
(Senecio keniensis)
ASTERACEAE FAMILY
3m ❀ **perennial**

Habitat Among tussock grasses in the
moorland, at altitudes above 2,400m.
Identification A woody plant
with a rosette of large (up to 40cm
long), broad leaves with slightly
upturned tips. They are green and
smooth above, with a white and
woolly undersurface (**1**) and with
entire margins. The 2–3m-tall,
branching inflorescence carries many
bright flowers.

Emilia discifolia
ASTERACEAE FAMILY
15cm ⚘ annual

Habitat Widespread at moderate altitude, on open ground and in rocky situations in dry bushland.
Identification An annual daisy that comes up after the rains, *E. discifolia* has hairy, spatula-like leaves **(1)** that are ovate, narrow, smooth at the base, rounded and toothed at the tip, with purplish margins. The flowers have darker yellow centres, and the stems are smooth, not hairy.

Euryops brownei
ASTERACEAE FAMILY
2m ⚘ perennial

Habitat High-altitude montane grassland and moorland.
Identification A tall, well-branched shrub with many narrow, needle-like leaves in an alternate arrangement along the stem. The bright yellow flowers are up to 2cm in width. May flower prolifically.
Notes Bees collect the pollen.

Haplocarpha rueppellii
ASTERACEAE FAMILY
5cm ◆ perennial

Habitat Along mountain streams and in open areas in high-altitude grassland.
Identification This small, compact daisy has a rosette **(1)** of broadly ovate leaves that lie close to the ground. The leaves are glossy, with a covering of soft, woolly hairs, and slightly wavy margins. Between four and five flowers, each up to 4cm across, open simultaneously.

Helichrysum odoratissimum
ASTERACEAE FAMILY
40cm ◆ perennial

Habitat High-altitude grassland; also, grassland and bush at moderate altitude.
Identification Tall and straggly, this plant is adorned with woolly hairs that give it a whitish appearance. The leaves are linear, with entire margins. Many small flowers are borne in compact flower heads **(1)**.
Notes When crushed, the flowers give off a strong scent reminiscent of curry powder.

Hirpicium diffusum
ASTERACEAE FAMILY
10cm ◆ annual

Habitat Disturbed ground and pockets of shallow soil in dry country, generally *Acacia* bushland.
Identification The leaves of this small, hairy annual vary in shape from linear and simple to pinnately lobed. The under surface is clothed in matted white hairs, while the upper surface is covered with rough hairs. The bright yellow-to-orange flowers are striking.

Kleinia odora
ASTERACEAE FAMILY
1m ◆ perennial

Habitat At moderate altitude in dry *Acacia-Commiphora* bushland.
Identification A shrub with zigzagging, faintly striped (1) stems up to 3cm in width. The name *odora* is a reference to the distinct pleasant smell of the stems when broken. (In *K. squarrosa*, by contrast, the broken stems have a rather unpleasant odour.) The leaves are ovate, small and fleshy, and the white-to-yellowish flowers are borne in bunches.
Notes Butterflies feed from this plant, as do many other insects.

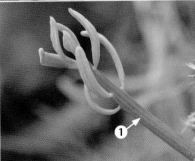

Osteospermum vaillantii

ASTERACEAE FAMILY

40cm ◆ perennial

Habitat Bare ground in arid areas, where it is very widespread.

Identification An upright herb with multiple branches sprouting from the base. The leaves are lanceolate and toothed, with soft hairs. The yellow flowers are 2cm across. When unripe, the seed pods **(1)** have purple streaks that become translucent as they dry out. The entire plant is sticky and glandular, and the leaves are aromatic when crushed.

Psiadia punctulata

ASTERACEAE FAMILY

1.5m ◆ perennial

Habitat Widespread from the coast to areas at moderate altitude further inland. May be abundant on plots (*shambas*) where the bush has been cleared for cultivation, but generally forms smaller stands in undisturbed bushland.

Identification A rounded herb or shrub with lanceolate, entire, shiny green leaves that are covered in glandular hairs and are sticky when crushed. The flowers are small, in heads 6—8cm across.

Notes The leaves are heated over hot coals and pressed onto aching muscles to provide relief. The plant also has insect-repellent properties, and leafy branches are traditionally used to sweep earthen floors to keep fleas away.

Senecio hadiensis
ASTERACEAE FAMILY
10m ◈ perennial

Habitat The margins of dry cedar-olive forest.
Identification A tough climber that may completely cover a tree. It is semi-succulent, with alternately arranged, broadly elliptical, hairless and slightly toothed leaves **(1)**. Conspicuous bunches of (mostly five-petalled) flowers are borne at the tops of branches.
Notes This plant is well loved by insects, particularly flies and beetles. It makes a useful and attractive garden plant that can be grown along a fence or trained as a hedge.

Solanecio cydoniifolius
ASTERACEAE FAMILY
4m ◈ perennial

Habitat Widespread in coastal belt vegetation, on the margins of upland forest, in dry cedar-olive forest and in *Acacia* bushland.
Identification A thick-stemmed climber with long, broadly ovate leaves covered in woolly white hairs. The leaves are 20cm or more in length, with entire margins. The yellow flowers are borne on a stem that branches two or three times. They are compact and narrow (up to 1cm wide).

Solanecio mannii
ASTERACEAE FAMILY
3m ◆ perennial

Habitat Abundant in montane forest, often where trees have been cleared; also found in hedges surrounding cultivated plots (*shambas*).
Identification A tall plant with straight stems and long (up to 30cm), toothed, lanceolate leaves that form a rosette. The inflorescence is tall and branched and carries many flowers.

Taraxacum officinale
ASTERACEAE FAMILY
10cm ◆ perennial

Habitat An exotic from Europe, this plant has now become naturalised in most areas of upland grassland and among short grasses growing along forest margins.
Identification A hairy herb that lies close to the ground and bears long dark green leaves that are pinnate and lobed. Bright flowers are carried in dense heads measuring about 3cm across.

81

Heliotropium zeylanicum
BORAGINACEAE FAMILY
20cm ❀ **perennial**

Habitat Bare ground in dry bushland.
Identification This small herb has softly
hairy, narrow, elliptical leaves with
slightly wavy margins. The flowers **(1)**
are cream coloured, arranged alternately
up the stem, resembling small stars. The
petals are very thin, and the flowering
stems are clothed in white hairs.

Chamaecrista fallacina
(Cassia fallacina)
CAESALPINIACEAE FAMILY
4cm ❀ **perennial**

Habitat Bare patches in dry bushland
and open grassland.
Identification A small, hairy,
widespread herb that creeps along the
ground. The leaves comprise many
asymmetrical leaflets with red-tinged
margins. Nectar-bearing glands are
found at the base of the leaves. The
flowers are small – just 2cm across.

Tylosema fassoglense
CAESALPINIACEAE FAMILY
1m ◈ **perennial**

Habitat Bare, open ground in dry country, at altitudes below about 1,500m.
Identification A perennial climber with a large underground tuber. The leaves are rounded to heart-shaped and up to 10cm in width; they emerge after the flowers, during the rains. Several racemes sprout at once from the tuberous root, each carrying up to 20 buds **(1)**. The flowers have papery petals. The seed pods are edible.

Cleome angustifolia
CLEOMACEAE FAMILY
15cm ◈ **annual**

Habitat Hot semi-desert areas.
Identification A tall, hairless herb with palmate leaves comprising 4–9 very narrow leaflets. The flowers are a striking bright yellow, with a reddish-orange base, and have two large back petals **(1)** and two smaller front petals. The seed pod is straight, narrow and measures up to 6cm.

Combretum falcatum
COMBRETACEAE FAMILY
10m ◆ perennial

Habitat Coastal forests and coastal-belt bushland.
Identification A scrambling shrub or climber with entire, ovate leaves (4–6cm long). Bunches of flowers emerge from leafy bracts. Their floral tubes measure up to 3cm.
Notes Butterflies frequent the flowers.

Commelina africana
COMMELINACEAE FAMILY
8cm ◆ perennial

Habitat Widespread from dry bushland along the coastal belt to *Acacia* bushland at moderate altitude.
Identification Among the smallest *Commelina* species, this plant varies in size and colour. It creeps along the ground and has long, hairy leaves that fold slightly inwards. The flowers are just 2cm across. They are enclosed in a single spathe.

Ipomoea obscura
CONVOLVULACEAE FAMILY
3m ◆ **perennial**

Habitat At moderate altitude in dry bushland and along forest margins.
Identification A small, delicate climber that has smooth, heart-shaped leaves with entire margins. Many yellow to orange flowers are borne along the stems. They are about 4cm across with markings that form a star shape **(1)**.

Merremia ampelophylla
CONVOLVULACEAE FAMILY
2cm ◆ **perennial**

Habitat Bare ground in dry *Acacia-Commiphora* bushland; also found in seasonal gullies (*luggas*) and riverbeds.
Identification This creeping herb has hairy, palmate leaves with 5–7 unevenly toothed lobes. The flowers are 5cm across, with five shallow lobes.
Notes An attractive dryland creeper that brightens up bare ground.

Kalanchoe citrina
CRASSULACEAE FAMILY
40cm ◆ perennial

Habitat Dry bushland at low to moderate altitude.
Identification An upright herb with leaves arranged alternately around the stem. The leaves **(1)** are lanceolate, fleshy and strongly toothed, up to 5cm in length, and are covered in soft hairs. Flowers, 0.8–1cm long, are carried in dense clusters at the tops of flowering stems.
Notes This species is pollinated mainly by butterflies.

Kalanchoe densiflora
CRASSULACEAE FAMILY
1m ◆ perennial

Habitat At moderate to high altitude, along forest edges and in grassland.
Identification This smooth, hairless succulent has large, circular, fleshy leaves with toothed margins. The flowers, which are up to 1.2cm long, are carried in heads 7–10cm across and are larger and a richer yellow than those of *K. citrina*. The petals are squared off, but with a central point.

Kalanchoe glaucescens
CRASSULACEAE FAMILY
30cm ◆ **perennial**

Habitat Most types of dry bushland.
Favours shallow soil overlying
rocky ground.
Identification This smooth succulent
has greyish leaves with purple
markings **(1)** along the toothed margins.
The creamy yellow flowers, which are
loosely arranged in a head, are up to
1.2cm long, with narrow petals.

Kalanchoe mitejea
CRASSULACEAE FAMILY
3m ◆ **perennial**

Habitat Dry bushland, often within
the shelter of a shrub or tree.
Identification This tall succulent has
inward-folding, boat-shaped leaves,
with a smooth green upper surface
and a mottled purple undersurface.
The flowers, carried on inflated flower
tubes (pedicels) **(1)** up to 2.5cm
long, are loosely arranged in heads.
This species has among the largest
inflorescences of any *Kalanchoe*.

Sedum ruwenzoriense
CRASSULACEAE FAMILY
10cm ◆ perennial

Habitat Rocky crevices in montane grassland.
Identification This fairly robust herb may be upright or trailing. Tightly packed along the warty grey stems (**1**), the leaves are fleshy and green, with some reddish-purple markings. They are short (about 1cm long) and rounded. The flowers, too, are small, just 1cm across.

Coccinea grandis
CUCURBITACEAE FAMILY
10m ◆ perennial

Habitat Dry cedar-olive forest and the margins of seasonal streams and gullies (*luggas*) in hot, dry country.
Identification A widespread climber with large, hairy, pinnate leaves divided into five lobes. The venation gives a bumpy appearance to the upper surface of the leaf. There is a gland at the base of each leaf and glandular hairs cover the stems (**1**). The flowers are large (up to 7cm across) and the fruits (**2**) are elongated, turning orange when ripe. The seeds inside – but not the surrounding pulp – are edible.
Notes Monkeys and birds enjoy eating the fruit.

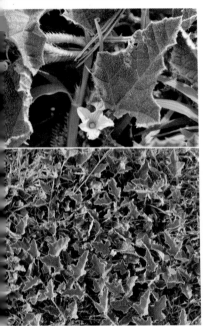

Cucumis aculeatus
CUCURBITACEAE FAMILY
3m ◆ **perennial**

Habitat At moderate altitude in dry bushland and open grassland.
Identification A widespread, creeping curcurbit with hooked hairs on the stems, and ovate, hairy, lobed, greyish-green leaves with a very rough texture. The flowers are small (2cm across), and the fruits **(1)** are knobbly and green, turning yellow when ripe.
Notes The flowers are well loved by bees.

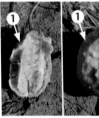

Euphorbia glochidiata
EUPHORBIACEAE FAMILY
60cm ◆ **perennial**

Habitat Dry *Acacia-Commiphora* bushland.
Identification An upright *Euphorbia* with small, angular stems **(1)**, which are variegated in purple and green. Small (0.4cm) and large (0.8cm) spines are borne on grey spine shields. Tiny yellow to red flowers (up to 0.4cm across) are carried in groups of three along the angled stem margins.
Notes The variegated stem makes this an attractive plant that is valued by collectors. It is suitable for planting in a pot.

Euphorbia gossypina
EUPHORBIACEAE FAMILY
10m ◈ perennial

Habitat Widespread in dry, rocky areas and *Acacia* bushland.
Identification A fleshy shrub with milky latex. The greenish stems often have tinges of pink or purple. The narrow leaves usually dry out and drop off quite quickly. About five to eight flowers are borne in each umbel **(1)**.
Notes Beetles enjoy eating the flowers.

Euphorbia laikipiensis
EUPHORBIACEAE FAMILY
8cm ◈ perennial

Habitat Fairly common in pockets of shallow soil overlying rock.
Identification A compact little *Euphorbia* with dense creeping stems up to 10cm in length. It carries twinned greyish spines **(1)** on spine shields. Small flowers (0.6cm across) are carried close to the stem.
Notes In areas with a high density of wildlife the plant is well browsed. The entire plant can be roasted to neutralise the poisonous latex and then boiled up and used as medicine for coughs and colds.

Euphorbia samburuensis
EUPHORBIACEAE FAMILY
10cm ◆ perennial

Habitat Open semi-desert country.
Identification A small, robust, spiny *Euphorbia* with no leaves. The stems **(1)** are pale purplish to greenish, marked with white lines, and carry many paired, 2cm-long, pale grey spines. The small flowers are carried in groups at the tops of stems. They often glisten with nectar that attracts ants and other insects. The seed capsules are small and four-sided.

Flagellaria indica
FLAGELLERIACEAE FAMILY
10m ◆ perennial

Habitat Coastal bush and forest.
Identification Although this forest climber has grass-like leaves and stems and is easily mistaken for bamboo or another species of grass, it in fact belongs in its own family. The leaves, which are glossy and smooth, have tendrils at their tips, which help them to scramble up into the trees. The pale yellow to white flowers are carried at the tops of the branches and are small (0.4–0.5cm long). The bunches of berries **(1)** ripen to a shiny red and are edible.
Notes The split stems are used to weave very strong baskets.

Monsonia longipes
GERANACEAE FAMILY
5cm ◆ perennial

Habitat Pockets of shallow soil
in rocky *Acacia* bushland, at
moderate altitude.
Identification A small herb with
spreading branches, *M. longipes* tends
to creep along the ground. The stems
are hairy, and the leaves have wavy
margins, purplish markings on the
upper surface and two lobes at the
base. The lemony to bright yellow
flowers are 4cm wide, with five petals.

Albuca abyssinica
HYACINTHACEAE FAMILY
40cm ◆ perennial

Habitat Dry areas in open grassland
and bushland, at moderate altitude.
Identification A lily that
arises from a rounded
underground bulb.
The leaves are flat, up
to 12cm long and 3cm
wide, and exude a glue-
like substance when
broken. The inflorescence
varies from 20–70cm in
height, depending on the
conditions. The flowers
are bell-shaped and
pendent and vary from
yellow or cream to green,
with a green midrib.

Ottelia ulvifolia
HYDROCHARITACEAE FAMILY
1m ◆ **perennial**

Habitat Dams, seasonal pools and other waterbodies.
Identification An aquatic plant with large, strappy leaves that are often submerged. They are broad, up to 10cm long and taper to a narrow tip. Bright yellow flowers are borne above the water and measure about 5cm across.

Hypericum revolutum
HYPERICACEAE FAMILY
3.5m ◆ **perennial**

Habitat Upland forest and relict forest at higher altitude.
Identification *H. revolutum* is probably the most abundant member of this upland forest genus. The leaves are glandular, opposite and narrow, with entire margins, and are closely arranged along the stems. The flowers are up to 5cm across, very showy, with five widely spaced petals that tend to persist for some time.
Notes When they're encountered in a habitat that seems unusual for a *Hypericum*, it is often a sign that forest once occurred there.

Hypoxis obtusa
HYPOXIDACEAE FAMILY
9cm ◇ perennial

Habitat Areas of shallow, rocky soil at moderate altitude.
Identification A small herb with a large, potato-like root that is yellow or orange when cut open. The leaves are narrow, slightly recurved, up to 6cm long, and clothed in soft white hairs (1). The flowers have six spreading petals and are carried on a short stem. Several flowers open at the same time.
Notes The large yellow roots are edible and are used medicinally in southern Africa to treat many different ailments. This plant is protected in some parts of that region.

Plicosepalus curviflorus
LORANTHACEAE FAMILY
1m ◇ perennial

Habitat *Acacia-Commiphora* bushland, where it parasitises mainly *Acacia* species.
Identification This very striking parasitic plant is conspicuous in dry bushland. Its stems are rough, with small, raised bumps, and its leaves, which are oval, greyish, smooth and slightly succulent, with entire margins, are carried in bunches close to the stem. The reddish stamens are upturned, and the yellow petals (1) are narrow and strongly curling. The seeds are oval, turning red when ripe.

Caucanthus auriculatus
MALPIGHIACEAE FAMILY
10m ◆ **perennial**

Habitat Semi-arid bushland, rocky hills and the margins of well-vegetated seasonal streams in *Acacia-Commiphora* country.
Identification A climber with broadly ovate leaves, which are up to 10cm long and clothed in soft, appressed hairs, particularly on the under surface. The pale yellow flowers are 2cm across with five petals and are densely bunched. They are conspicuous in dry bush.

Abutilon mauritianum
MALVACEAE FAMILY
1m ◆ **perennial/annual**

Habitat Deep shade in dry areas, often on disturbed ground.
Identification A woody plant with alternately arranged, heart-shaped leaves, deeply notched at the base and with toothed margins. The flowers measure 3–4cm across and are carried on a hairy flowering stem. The fruit (1) is an attractive disc that splits open when the seeds are dry. The seeds are edible, as are the flowers.

Hibiscus calyphyllus
MALVACEAE FAMILY
80cm ❖ perennial

Habitat At moderate altitude, generally in shaded situations, in a range of habitats, from dry bushland to forest margins.
Identification This herb or shrub can become quite tall. The leaves have toothed margins and are ovate, sometimes with 2–3 quite small lobes. Close inspection reveals star-shaped hairs on the leaf surface. The flowers are large, bright and up to 10cm wide. They open only when the sun is shining.
Notes Both leaves and petals are edible.

Hibiscus physaloides
MALVACEAE FAMILY
2m ❖ perennial

Habitat Along roadsides and on forest margins at the coastal belt; also extends slightly inland.
Identification This tall perennial has hairy leaves with three lobes. The central lobe is longest, at 4cm. Irritating hairs cover the stems, leaves and buds. The flowers measure 10–12cm across, and the petals each have a small tooth **(1)**, making them appear slightly asymmetrical.

Hibiscus trionum
MALVACEAE FAMILY
5cm ◆ annual

Habitat *Acacia* grassland. Favours black cotton soils at moderate altitude and often occurs near standing water, such as seasonal pans.
Identification A low-lying herb that creeps along the ground, this *Hibiscus* has deeply lobed leaves with purplish margins **(1)** and a covering of soft hairs. The flowers are up to 6cm across, pale yellowish, with a deep purple centre and hairy sepals. The seed pods have attractive purple stripes.
Notes Both the seeds and petals are edible.

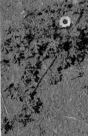

Hibiscus vitifolius
MALVACEAE FAMILY
1m ◆ perennial

Habitat In sheltered situations on rocky escarpments and along forest margins.
Identification A loose herb or shrub that branches from the base. The stems and leaves are covered with irritating glandular hairs. The leaves are triangular and may have 3–4 lobes. The flowers are pendent, yellow with a purple centre, and do not open fully. In very arid areas they tend to be mauve. The seed pod is hairy.

Melhania velutina
MALVACEAE FAMILY
40cm · perennial

Habitat In shallow soil overlying rock in dry bushland.
Identification An upright herb with rust-coloured, hairy shoots that become paler with age. The leaves are ovate to elliptical, covered in rust-coloured hairs, and up to 5cm long. Flowers are borne in clusters 1.5cm across and are followed by very hairy fruits.

Pavonia burchellii
MALVACEAE FAMILY
40cm · perennial/annual

Habitat Varied; from semi-arid areas to forest margins. Usually found in dense shade.
Identification A softly hairy, mostly upright plant with rounded, irregularly lobed **(1)** leaves that have toothed margins. Flowers up to 3cm across emerge from the leaf axils on a delicate, 4cm-long stalk.
Notes Bees collect pollen from the flowers.

Pavonia gallaensis

MALVACEAE FAMILY

10cm   perennial

Habitat Grassland at moderate altitude.
Identification An abundant and
pretty little plant with greyish leaves,
which are broadly ovate with toothed
margins **(1)** and covered in dense,
soft hairs. The flowers are small, about
2cm across, with five petals. The outer
sepals are softly hairy.

Sida cordifolia

MALVACEAE FAMILY

17cm   annual

Habitat Fairly widespread in
dry bushland.
Identification A tough herb with
woody stems. The leaves are ovate,
with serrated margins **(1)**, and are
covered in short hairs. The flowers are
small, up to 2cm across.

Sida tenuicarpa
MALVACEAE FAMILY
1m ◈ **perennial**

Habitat Widespread in upland grassland and in dry *Acacia* bushland.
Identification This very tough, squat herb has small, smooth leaves that are linear and up to 2cm long; there is a notch at the tip of the leaf. The flowers are bright yellow with darker orange streaks.
Notes The branches are traditionally used as brushes for sweeping.

Triumfetta rhomboidea
MALVACEAE FAMILY
80cm ◈ **perennial**

Habitat A regular feature along roadsides and in disturbed ground, this plant is also found along forest edges at moderate altitude.
Identification An upright herb that has ovate, usually three-lobed leaves, which are rough to the touch. The flowers are small (0.5cm across) and are carried in bunches. Prickles cover the oblong, whitish fruits.

Ludwigia adscendens (L. stolonifera)
ONAGRACEAE FAMILY
6cm ◆ perennial

Habitat Dams, streams and rivers, where it floats on the water surface.
Identification This aquatic plant has smooth, lanceolate leaves with purple-tinged edges and entire margins. The plant roots itself and then floats on top of the water, remaining buoyant thanks to spongy white floating roots (1). The flowers have five petals.

Ansellia africana
ORCHIDACEAE FAMILY
1m ◆ perennial

Habitat Epiphytic on other plants in *Acacia-Combretum* woodland. In some areas, such as *Acacia* bushland, it is abundant as a ground orchid.
Identification One of the most beautiful orchids in the region, this plant is threatened by loss of habitat and overexploitation by collectors. It has strong, upright, bamboo-like stems and erect, ribbed leaves. The inflorescence is a large panicle

bearing many yellowish-green flowers, marked with deep purplish-brown spots. The flowers are pollinated by carpenter bees.

Eulophia orthoplectra
ORCHIDACEAE FAMILY
1m ◆ perennial

Habitat Grassland at altitudes of between 1,500 and 1,800m.
Identification This rare species arises from an underground bulb. The leaves are long, often bend over and are fleshy, rather than leathery like those of *E. petersii* (below). The sepals are reddish and recurved, and the petals are bright yellow.

Eulophia petersii
ORCHIDACEAE FAMILY
1.1m ◆ perennial

Habitat Widespread and occurs at a range of altitudes, from sand dunes on the coastal belt to rocky upland areas.
Identification This species arises from an above-ground, bottle-shaped tuber. The leaves are thick and leathery, with a rough surface texture and small marginal teeth. The flower has three backward-curving yellow-green sepals (1), and the petals are the same colour, with faint brown stripes, except for the lower petal, which is white with pink markings.

BL

Eulophia speciosa
ORCHIDACEAE FAMILY
1.5m ◆ perennial

Habitat This ground orchid occurs in dry bushland and along the coastal belt.
Identification Like other *Eulophia* species, it arises from an underground rhizome and flowers when it rains. The long leaves often emerge only after flowering. The flowering stem attains about a metre and is adorned with up to 20 flowers with rounded petals and recurved sepals.

Eulophia stenophylla
ORCHIDACEAE FAMILY
2m ◆ perennial

Habitat Dry bushland and rocky areas.
Identification A ground orchid with an above-ground pseudobulb (bulb-like stem enlargement). The leaves emerge with the flowers and are just 2cm across. The flowers are borne in a raceme and have rounded petals and large, forward-facing, greenish sepals (1), with some brown markings.

Orthochilus mechowii
(Eulophia zeyheri)
ORCHIDACEAE FAMILY
65cm   perennial

Habitat Open grassland, mainly in western Kenya.
Identification An attractive ground orchid whose long, narrow leaves emerge with the flowers, which are crowded at the top of the stem and have open, pale petals. The lower petal has small central hairs.

Polystachya campyloglossa
ORCHIDACEAE FAMILY
10cm   perennial

Habitat Mossy tree branches in dry cedar-olive forest.
Identification A small orchid with a short pseudobulb (stem enlargement) at the base of the stem. The leaves are lanceolate, with a slightly pointed tip, and measure up to 6cm in length. The flowering stem carries 3–6 greenish-yellow flowers with a white lip marked with purple spots.

Cistanche tubulosa
OROBANCHACEAE FAMILY
10cm ◆ **perennial**

Habitat In arid bushland, wherever suitable host plants occur.
Identification This upright herb lacks chlorophyll and must parasitise the roots of a tree or shrub to obtain nutrients. Bright flowers are carried on an upright spike. The flowers emerge from scale-like bracts **(1)**, and the sepals have five lobes.

Crotalaria agatiflora
PAPILIONACEAE FAMILY
2m ◆ **perennial**

Habitat Generally at moderate to high altitude, where it is widespread along roadsides, forest edges, rivers and streams.
Identification A tall herb or shrub with bunches of dark green compound leaves, each comprising three leaflets. The leaflets are narrow but broader in the middle and up to 6cm long. The large, greenish yellow, showy flowers are arranged alternately on a long raceme, and have hairy, purplish-green sepals **(1)**. The seed pods are hard when dry and up to 5cm in length.

Crotalaria laburnifolia subsp. *laburnifolia*

PAPILIONACEAE FAMILY
70cm ✦ perennial

Habitat Along roadsides in open grassland and bushland, at moderate to low altitude.
Identification A widespread, pretty and variable plant. Several may be found growing together. The main stems are pale pink, and the leaves, which are greyish-green, comprise three broadly ovate leaflets, each with a slightly pointed tip. The flowers are borne in a long raceme and deepen in colour from yellow-orange once pollinated. The seed pods are about 5cm long. Three subspecies are known.

Crotalaria pycnostachya

PAPILIONACEAE FAMILY
80cm ✦ annual

Habitat On sand dunes along the coastal belt and in dry inland habitats, such as *Acacia-Commiphora* woodland.
Identification An upright, bushy herb with hairy branches. The leaves **(1)** consist of three narrow leaflets, each up to 4cm long. Small flowers appear in bunches carried on a short raceme. The pods are club-shaped, up to 1.5cm long and covered in tiny hairs.

Crotalaria retusa
PAPILIONACEAE FAMILY
80cm ◈ perennial

Habitat Along the coastal belt and on forest margins.
Identification A small herb branching at right angles to the main stem. The simple, eliptical leaves (1) have a few hairs on the upper surface and many appressed hairs on the lower surface. Leaf margins are entire. Tightly bunched flowers are yellow, veined purplish (2), borne on a short, 10-cm spike; the flower stalk has short hairs. The pods (3), up to 4cm long, are yellowish to brown when ripe.

Rhynchosia holstii
PAPILIONACEAE FAMILY
3cm ◈ annual

Habitat Areas of black cotton soil, in *Acacia* grassland; also favours rocky habitats.
Identification This is a creeping plant with compound leaves comprising three obovate leaflets with entire margins and some greyish hairs on the upper surface. The flowers are alternately arranged in a raceme about 7cm long. The pretty yellow buds are marked with reddish lines.

Sophora inhambanensis
PAPILIONACEAE FAMILY
1.5m ◆ perennial

Habitat On the coastal belt, usually just beyond the beach, close to the dunes.
Identification A leafy shrub whose leaves are covered in short, silky hairs that give it a lovely silver-grey appearance. The leaves are pinnate, with up to seven pairs of leaflets. Flowers are borne at the tops of the branches, and the seed pods (1) are constricted. The seeds are hard when dry, rounded and up to 2cm in width.

Zornia setosa
PAPILIONACEAE FAMILY
4cm ◆ perennial

Habitat Sandy, granitic soils in *Acacia* bushland.
Identification A trailing herb with short, compound leaves. Each of the four leaflets is 1–2cm long, obovate with marginal hairs. The flowers are about 1cm across, with reddish streaks (1) on the upper petal and leaf-like bracts.

Pedalium murex
PEDALIACEAE FAMILY
70cm ◆ annual

Habitat Bare and disturbed ground along the coastal belt.
Identification A leafy, somewhat hairy herb with elliptical, obovate and slightly succulent leaves that have coarsely toothed margins. The flowers are pale, with soft hairs in the throat, and the fruit (**1**) has four soft spines.
Notes The leaves can be eaten as a vegetable.

Pterodiscus ruspolii
PEDALIACEAE FAMILY
10cm ◆ perennial

Habitat Semi-arid areas of rocky ground in *Acacia-Commiphora* bushland.
Identification A compact herb with leaves on long stalks. The leaves are dark green and ovate, with entire margins. Five-petalled flowers are arranged at the tips of leafy stems.

Portulaca quadrifidia
PORTULACACEAE FAMILY
2cm ❖ annual

Habitat Bare ground in dry bushland and open grassy glades.
Identification A creeping herb that may cover large areas. The stems have scales and long white hairs at the nodes and bear short, narrow, fleshy leaves measuring about 1cm. When it gets hot, the leaves fold against the stem. They also turn purple when growing in a sunny position. The flowers are bright, with four petals, and measure up to 2cm across.
Notes An important source of pollen for bees.

Rhabdotosperma brevipedicellata (Verbascum brevipedicellatum)
SCROPHULARIACEAE FAMILY
1.5m ❖ perennial

Habitat The margins of montane forest; also in upland grassland.
Identification This tall plant has stalkless leaves that alternate along the deep purple stems. They are lanceolate with toothed margins. Flowers with five petals are alternately arranged around the long, whispy racemes (**1**), which arise from the base of the plant. Both the sepals and the stems have a covering of glandular white hairs.

Verbascum sinaiticum
SCROPHULARIACEAE FAMILY
1.5m ◆ **perennial**

Habitat At altitudes below about 8,400m, on the margins of cedar-olive forest, along roadsides and in ditches.
Identification A tall plant with a broad rosette (**1**) of densely hairy, greyish leaves, each about 30cm, with wavy, toothed margins. The outer leaves at the base are stalkless. The inflorescence is tall and branches halfway up, with flowers arranged closely together along its length. The blooms have four petals and dense hairs on the stamens.

Withania somnifera
SOLANACEAE FAMILY
40cm ◆ **perennial**

Habitat Although this species originated in Asia, it has long been naturalised in East Africa. Often found in disturbed ground.
Identification A bushy herb with soft white hairs on all parts of the plant. It has soft, ovate leaves up to 10cm long, with slightly wavy margins. When crushed, the leaves emit a bitter smell. The yellow-green flowers (**1**) are small (just 0.4cm across), and the fruit (**2**) is enclosed in a papery skin, which turns bright reddish-orange when ripe.
Note Birds enjoy eating the fruits. The root is used in *ashwaganda*, an Ayurvedic medicine believed to boost immunity.

Tribulus cistoides
ZYGOPHYLLACEAE FAMILY
10cm ◈ annual

Habitat Semi-arid *Acacia-Commiphora* bushland, at low altitude.
Identification A trailing plant that often covers large areas of bare ground. It is one of the first annuals to appear after rain in semi-arid regions and brightens up the otherwise bleak landscape with its large flowers. The leaves are compound with many leaflets, which are more pointed than those of *T. terrestris* but equally hairy. The flowers are about 2.5cm across. The fruits are covered in sharp spines.

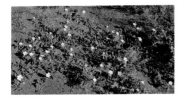

Tribulus terrestris
ZYGOPHYLLACEAE FAMILY
10cm ◈ annual

Habitat Widespread in *Acacia* bushland at higher altitude and in semi-arid to arid bushland at lower altitude. It favours bare, open ground.
Identification A small creeper covered in short, white hairs. The leaves **(1)** are pinnate, comprising 18 or more leaflets. The flowers are small (about 1.5cm in diameter). It is known as 'devil thorn' for the tough-horned spines that cover the oblong fruits and that have pierced countless feet.
Notes In semi-arid areas pastoralists depend on this plant as fodder for their livestock, which roam and graze freely.

Crossandra massaica
ACANTHACEAE FAMILY
10cm ◆ perennial

Habitat Dry bushland at moderate altitude; also dry cedar-olive forest; tends to prefer rocky locations.
Identification A straggly, compact herb that generally grows close to the ground, but sometimes scrambles up into nearby vegetation, in which case it can attain a metre in height. Its leaves vary from elliptical to broadly ovate. They tend to be darker green when growing in shaded positions. The flowers are striking, appearing soon after the first rains and brightening up the otherwise nondescript bushland. They emerge from softly pointed leafy bracts (1), which sheath a short flowering stalk. Bright coral red with up to five lobes, they look as though they've been cut in half.

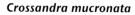

Crossandra mucronata
ACANTHACEAE FAMILY
20cm ◆ perennial

Habitat Semi-shaded positions in dry *Acacia* bushland. Favours exposed soils in open, rocky areas.
Identification This *Crossandra* occurs at lower altitude than *C. massaica* and is more compact. It has narrow leaves measuring up to 6cm in length. The flowering stems emerge from the base of the plant and are also clothed in leafy bracts, but these are harder, with a sharper point (1) than those of *C. massaica*. The flowers are paler and more orange than coral.

Crossandra subacaulis
ACANTHACEAE FAMILY
10cm ◆ perennial

Habitat Wooded grassland.
Identification A small plant with a rosette of leaves pressed almost flat to the ground. The leaves are stalkless, dark green, up to 15cm long and have wavy margins **(1)**. Pale orange flowers up to 4cm long are carried in a flowering head. The bracts are softly hairy, with a spike at the tip.

Thunbergia alata
ACANTHACEAE FAMILY
3m ◆ perennial

Habitat Thickets in dry bushland or grassland. A purple-throated white variety is found climbing over dry rocky outcrops.
Identification A climber with twining stems. It has triangular leaves, with toothed margins and winged petioles, hence the Latin name *alata*, which means 'wings'. Plants may have orange, yellow or white flowers, always with a purplish centre. The seeds are woody and ridged.

Thunbergia gregorii
ACANTHACEAE FAMILY
3m ◆ perennial

Habitat Confined to grassland at higher altitude.
Identification A trailing herb with broadly lanceolate to triangular leaves up to 5cm long. The stems are covered with bristly orange hairs. It carries solitary flowers that are larger than those of *T. alata*.
Notes *Thunbergia* species make attractive and rewarding garden plants.

Gloriosa superba var. *graminifolia (G. minor)*
AMARYLLIDACEAE FAMILY
15cm ◆ perennial

Habitat Semi-arid and desert areas.
Identification Unlike its relative *G. superba* var. *superba* (p.128), which climbs by means of leaf-tip tendrils, this small, dry-country plant lacks such tendrils and remains close to the ground. Its leaves are narrow, often fold inward and are arranged tightly around the stem. The flowers vary in colour from pale orange to dark red and are smaller than those of *G. s.* var. *superba*.
Notes The corm (bulb) is poisonous.

Orbea laikipiensis
APOCYNACEAE FAMILY
4cm ◆ perennial

Habitat Open grassland, among
clumps of grass and on rocky ground.
Identification Although this plant
is locally common, it is cryptic and
may be difficult to spot. The stems
are variegated, up to 3cm thick and
covered with short, pointed lobes.
The flowers have narrow petal-like
lobes and a yellow centre.

Aloe archeri
ASPHODELACEAE FAMILY
1m ◆ perennial

Habitat Shaded or semi-shaded
positions in semi-arid *Acacia* bushland.
Identification A clump-forming plant
that comprises a rosette of toothed,
red-brown (in sunny positions) to green
(in shaded positions) leaves that are
alternately arranged around a short,
concealed central stem. It may grow
unsupported, or lean against a tree.
The inflorescence is tall (up to a metre)
and branching with
orange to salmon
pink flowers arranged
in a dense raceme.
There are large bracts
on the buds. The
seeds are enclosed in
a dry capsule.
Notes Sunbirds
enjoy feeding from
the flowers.

Aloe elgonica

ASPHODELACEAE FAMILY

1m ◆ perennial

Habitat Western Kenya, on the rocky lower slopes of Mt Elgon and at Eldoret. Often hangs over rocky shelves.
Identification This succulent branches from its base, producing clumps of leafy stems up to 1m tall. The leaves, 50cm x 10cm, have very rough marginal teeth. A branching inflorescence of up to 60cm carries the reddish orange flowers.

Aloe ellenbeckii (A. dumetorum)

ASPHODELACEAE FAMILY

35cm ◆ perennial

Habitat Semi-arid areas on rocky, well-drained soils, mostly in shaded situations.
Identification A succulent plant that tends to form dense stands. The leaves are 3–4cm wide, 10–12cm long and are arranged in a rosette. They have white spots on the upper surface, toothed margins, are fleshy and contain a gel-like substance. A single flowering stalk arises from the midst of the leaves, bearing a head of orange flowers at its tip.

Aloe lateritia var. *graminicola*
ASPHODELACEAE FAMILY
1m ◆ perennial

Habitat Open grassland, where it forms large stands; also, *Acacia* woodland, where it is more scattered.
Identification Mature plants send out suckers, which take root and produce a solitary rosette of flat, open, white-spotted leaves, measuring 20cm x 5–6cm. The leaves have brown marginal teeth (1) and contain a gel-like substance. Orange-red flowers are borne in a capitate inflorescence. The papery-winged seeds are released when the capsule dries out.
Notes The gel from the leaves is traditionally applied to alleviate sunburn.

Aloe kedongensis
ASPHODELACEAE FAMILY
2.5m ◆ perennial

Habitat Volcanic soils in rocky areas on the edge of the Rift Valley.
Identification A shrubby plant that forms dense thickets. The leaves are greyish-green, up to 50cm long and 9cm wide, with toothed margins (1). The flowers are carried in a long raceme (up to 70cm).
Notes Sunbirds are attracted to aloes like this one, for their nectar.

Aloe nyeriensis
ASPHODELACEAE FAMILY
2m ◆ perennial

Habitat Rocky semi-arid bushland, mostly in flat areas, but sometimes on kopjes and phonolite escarpments.
Identification Another shrubby aloe that forms thick clumps. The leaves curl backwards, are pale green, up to 36cm long and 6cm wide, with pale brown marginal teeth. The leafy flowering stalk branches up to six times and bears bright orange flowers in a capitate inflorescence.
Notes In some parts of Kenya this species is confined to rocky scarps, because of enthusiastic grazing by Greater Kudu.

Aloe rabaiensis
ASPHODELACEAE FAMILY
3m ◆ perennial

Habitat At low altitude in mixed open grassland and *Acacia-Commiphora* woodland, generally inland from the coastal belt.
Identification A tall, shrubby aloe with much larger leaves than those of *A. kedongensis*. The leaves are pale green with pink-tinged tips, smooth, up to 36cm long and 7cm wide. They have brown-tipped marginal teeth (**1**). The inflorescence is about 1m tall, branches up to six times and carries dark orange terminal flowers in a capitate arrangement. The stamens are exserted (**2**).

Aloe secundiflora
ASPHODELACEAE FAMILY
1m ◆ perennial

Habitat Dry *Acacia* bushland at moderate altitude.
Identification This widespread aloe may be solitary or reproduce by sending out suckers from its base. It has a large rosette of thick leaves, each about 40cm long, which are smooth and shiny, with thick brown marginal teeth. A tall inflorescence carries racemes of flowers arranged along only one side of each spreading branch (**1**). The seed pods are oval and soft, turning brown and releasing papery-winged seeds.
Notes Traditionally, the raw leaf sap has been applied topically to treat skin complaints. It has also been drunk as a tonic to boost immunity. The flowers are visited by sunbirds and bees.

Aloe volkensii
ASPHODELACEAE FAMILY
5m ◆ perennial

Habitat Dry bushland, often on rocky slopes.
Identification Tall and attractive, this is one of just a handful of tree aloes found in the region. It may branch from its base (**1**), producing greyish stems. A rosette of curved, toothed, grey-green leaves is borne at the top of the stem; older dead leaves usually persist (**2**) on the trunk below it. The inflorescence has up to 10 branches (**3**) bearing compact heads of orange flowers, paler at the tips.

Kniphofia thomsonii

ASPHODELACEAE FAMILY

2m ◆ perennial

Habitat Marshy moorland at high altitude; often forms pure stands among tussock grasses.

Identification A highly variable plant with fibrous rhizomes. Its leaves are loosely arranged at the base and are up to 1m long and 2cm wide. Plants in drier areas have keeled leaves. Flowers are carried in a raceme at the top of a single flowering stem of up to 2m, and are generally orange, sometimes yellow. They are widely spaced on the raceme, slightly curved and up to 4cm long. The unripe seed capsule is fleshy and ovoid.

Notes There are two recognised subspecies: *K. t. thomsonii*, which has hairless flowers, and *K. t. snowdenii*, in which the flowers are hirsute.

Kleinia petraea

ASTERACEAE FAMILY

7cm ◆ perennial

Habitat At higher altitude in open grassland and on bare, degraded ground.

Identification A tough, trailing succulent that is locally common and forms carpets on bare ground or among other plants in shaded situations. It has many fleshy, closely bunched, rounded, pale green leaves. Bright orange flowers form in heads at the tops of stems. The seeds **(1)** are adorned with soft, silky fibres that aid in wind dispersal.

Kleinia stapeliiformis
ASTERACEAE FAMILY
20cm ◆ perennial

Habitat In *Acacia* bushland
at moderate altitude; favours
rocky situations.
Identification A small, erect, hairless
herb. The stem is rounded and fleshy,
with attractive purple markings, and
the leaves are fleshy and linear. A
single, large, orange flower is borne
at the top of a long stem.
Notes This makes an attractive
potted plant.

Combretum constrictum
COMBRETACEAE FAMILY
10m ◆ perennial

Habitat Damp locations, such as
seasonal watercourses and pans at
lower altitude, either along the coastal
belt or among inland bushland.
Identification A many-branched
shrub or liana with shiny green leaves
that are sometimes arranged in groups
of three. As the leaf petioles mature,
they form a blunt, hooked spine.
The showy, reddish orange flowers
have small, narrow petals (1), long,
protruding stamens (2) and are carried
in rounded bunches that resemble
powder puffs. The fruits are winged.

Commelina reptans
COMMELINACEAE FAMILY
8cm ◆ perennial

Habitat Seasonal swamps and open grassland.
Identification A tuberous herb that creeps along, rooting at the nodes. The branches are erect when young, and the leaves are lanceolate, up to 4cm long, with slightly wavy margins. Pale peachy orange flowers 2.5cm in diameter are clasped by softly hairy spathes (**1**) with prominent venation.

Cotyledon barbeyi
CRASSULACEAE FAMILY
1m ◆ perennial

Habitat Dry, rocky hills, at a slightly higher elevation; also occurs in *Acacia* bushland.
Identification An upright plant with multiple stems. The leaves are fleshy, narrow to rounded, with a slightly powdery surface. The flowering stem is covered in glandular hairs, and about 15cm tall, with small, orange, bell-like flowers (**1**) (up to 2.5cm long) hanging in groups from its tip.

Kalanchoe ballyi
CRASSULACEAE FAMILY
20cm ◆ perennial

Habitat Bushland along the coastal belt; favours shaded positions.
Identification A compact succulent plant with broad, smooth, hairless leaves that are pale lime green when young, turning darker green later. The flowers have glandular sepals and a yellow throat and are crowded at the top of the flowering stem. They are rather striking for an indigenous *Kalanchoe* species.

Kalanchoe lanceolata
(K. schweinfurthii)
CRASSULACEAE FAMILY
40cm ◆ perennial

Habitat Semi-shaded positions in *Acacia* bushland and grassland; also found on rocky escarpments and kopjes.
Identification An upright herb that usually occurs in clumps. There are glandular hairs on the stem and on the ovate leaves. Yellow to orange flowers, each up to 1cm long, are carried in a dense flowering head at the top of the flowering stem.

Hydnora abyssinica

HYDNORACEAE FAMILY
20cm ◆ perennial

Habitat Bushland and woodland, especially close to *Acacia* species.
Identification This unusual, surprisingly abundant plant is a parasite. *Acacia*s are believed to serve as host plants. Its rhizome (underground stem) is tough, warty and up to 10cm thick. The tip of the large flower appears above ground after the first rains. It has thick sepals with up to four orange-red lobes. The inner flower is bright red and bristly **(1)** below and pale cream above. The seeds form underground and are surrounded by a jelly-like pulp.
Notes The Borana people collect and dry the roots for use in traditional medicine. The flower petals are eaten by both people and animals; certain species of antelope will eat them right down to soil level.

Gladiolus dalenii (G. natalensis, G. newii)

IRIDACEAE FAMILY
80cm ◆ perennial

Habitat Upland grassland; in drier parts it may occur only after very good rains.
Identification An attractive upright plant with tough, narrow leaves about 25cm long. Up to 10 yellow-throated, orange flowers emerge at a time along the main stem. The petals are marked with orange flecks **(1)**.

Leonotis nepetifolia

LAMIACEAE FAMILY

3m ❖ annual

Habitat Common on disturbed ground, especially in cultivated areas.
Identification A tall, woody annual, with drooping, narrowly ovate leaves with a pointed tip and toothed margins (**1**). The leaf stalks measure about 4cm. Orange flowers are borne in whorls at the top of the flowering stem, the petals clothed in hairs (**2**) up to 0.1cm long. The flower heads are spiky, especially when dry. *L. n.* var. *africana*, found in western Kenya, has broad, blunt leaves.
Notes The flowers are rich in nectar, as is typical of a *Leonotis*, and are popular with sunbirds.

Leonotis ocymifolia (*L. mollisima*)

LAMIACEAE FAMILY

5m ❖ perennial

Habitat Forest margins at higher altitude.
Identification This robust herb is much woodier than *L. nepetifolia*. It has square stems and rounded to lanceolate leaves, both covered in soft hairs. The leaf margins are evenly toothed. Bright orange flowers are borne spirally in heads arranged about 7cm apart along the top of the flowering stem. They have hairy petals and are generally orange, but in rare instances plants produce white flowers. *L. o.* var. *ocymifolia* has pointed leaves, while *L. o.* var. *raineriana* has circular leaves.

Phragmanthera usuiensis
LORANTHACEAE FAMILY
30cm ◆ perennial

Habitat Host trees, especially *Acacia* species, in grassland and riverine vegetation; also parasitises some exotics, such as pepper trees (*Schinus mole*).
Identification A robust parasite with boat-shaped leaves that fold slightly inward. Young leaves are russet, later turning green. The flowers, which are upright and closely spaced along the stem, have pretty, twisted green stamens that curl up like a spring (**1**). The seeds are blue. The entire plant is hairy: young leaves in particular are clothed with a very fine hairs and there are even soft orange hairs on the flowers.
Notes Despite the concerns of many gardeners, this parasite does not usually kill its host. The flowers are well loved by sunbirds for their nectar.

Abutilon hirtum
MALVACEAE FAMILY
2m ◆ perennial

Habitat In dry areas along roadsides and ditches and in other disturbed ground.
Identification A more or less woody herb or shrub with roundish, softly hairy leaves that taper to a point and have toothed margins. Flowers

up to 4cm across are borne in the leaf axils and at the tops of the branches. They are orange with a dark reddish-purple centre, but some plants produce plain orange flowers. The stems, petioles and flower stalks are clothed in short, soft, sticky hairs.

Polystachya bella
ORCHIDACEAE FAMILY
12cm ◆ perennial

Habitat Moist forest at much higher altitude than most other orchid species; usually found growing epiphytically on moss-covered branches.
Identification Grows from a pale yellowish oval bulb. It produces tough, upright, dark green leaves, and the flowering stem bears many closely spaced orange-yellow flowers, each up to 1cm across and covered with small hairs. This is one of the showiest *Polystachya* species.

Indigofera volkensii
PAPILIONACEAE FAMILY
30cm ◆ perennial

Habitat Dry situations in *Acacia-Commiphora* bushland.
Identification A fairly common plant. The stems, leaves and flowers are covered with short white hairs. The leaves are compound, with many alternating, lanceolate leaflets. The orangey pink flowers are borne in racemes up to 8cm long, carried at the tips of flowering stems, and the seeds are carried in a seed pod up to 1.6cm long.

Boophone disticha

AMARYLLIDACEAE FAMILY
40cm ◆ perennial

Habitat Rocky escarpments in *Acacia* bushland and open grassland.
Identification This plant arises from a large underground bulb that lies dormant for most of the year. Leaves and flowers are produced before and during the rains. The leaves are arranged in a fan, have slightly wavy margins, prominent veins, and are up to 3cm wide. Greyish-green at first, they turn darker green later. Many dark red flowers are carried in a rounded, umbrella-shaped inflorescence on a single 25cm-tall stem. The petals curl backward.

Cyrtanthus sanguineus

AMARYLLIDACEAE FAMILY
30cm ◆ perennial

Habitat Stands of *Acacia drepanolobium* on black cotton soils at moderate altitude. Also, on rocky outcrops in open grassland.
Identification This plant arises from a bulb situated above ground. It bears one or two bright red flowers, each up to 10cm long, with a yellow throat (1) and petals that curl backward. Its strappy basal leaves emerge only after flowering is complete. The related *C. s. salmonoides* (not shown) has paler orange or salmon-coloured petals.

Gloriosa superba var. *superba* (*G. superba*)

AMARYLLIDACEAE FAMILY
4m ◆ perennial

Habitat Various upland vegetation types; also in *Acacia* bushland. Favours wetter, cooler areas than *G. s.* var. *graminifolia*.

Identification A more robust lily than the dry-country *G. s.* var. *graminifolia*. It grows from a corm shaped like a crow's foot. The stalkless, glossy, broad-based leaves have tendrils at their tips (1), enabling the plant to climb by holding onto other plants for support. The flowers are spectacular after good rains: often over 10cm long, they are nodding and have six petals that curl backward (2). Colour varies with habitat: while most upland plants have red or orange flowers, the pure yellow form (3) is characteristic of drier, lower-lying regions.

Notes The corms are poisonous.

Scadoxus multiflorus

AMARYLLIDACEAE FAMILY
35cm ◆ perennial

Habitat Coral cliffs on the coastal belt, dry cedar-olive forests and dry *Acacia-Commiphora* bushland at moderate altitude.

Identification This very widespread plant arises from an underground bulb, and the emergence of its flowers is thought to herald rain. The leaves are glossy green, with small purple spots at the base (1), and usually appear after the scarlet flowers, which fade to pink. The two- to three-sided fruits resemble berries.

Notes This species is a good source of pollen for bees.

Ceropegia albisepta var. *robynsiana* (C. succulenta)
APOCYNACEAE FAMILY
10m ◆ perennial

Habitat The margins of dry forest; also occurs in *Acacia* bushland.
Identification This showy *Ceropegia* has a thick, succulent stem and broadly elliptical leaves with wavy margins, pale veins and a smooth, shiny upper surface. The flowers have reddish-purple spots and measure 2–3cm in length. Small purple hairs (1) clothe the petal lobes. Pods are produced in pairs and open when ripe. The seeds have long, silky hairs to aid wind dispersal.

Ceropegia aristolochiodes (C. seticorona)
APOCYNACEAE FAMILY
3m ◆ perennial

Habitat Dry bushland and open grassland.
Identification A fleshy climber that contains gel-like sap, visible when the stem is broken. The leaves are opposite, green in the shade and purplish when exposed to sunlight. Upright and variable, the flowers may be purple with pale yellow spots, or pale yellow with darker purple spots, and the tips of the petals fuse to form a rounded, cage-like structure. There are small purple hairs on the petals.
Notes Flies enter the tube, which is lined with small, stiff hairs, where they pollinate the flower. After pollination the hairs become lax, allowing trapped flies to exit the tube.

Ceropegia ballyana
APOCYNACEAE FAMILY
3m ◆ perennial

Habitat Dry *Acacia* bushland, usually within the shelter of a tree, shrub or bush.
Identification Generally well hidden among thick bush, this is a fleshy climber with a relatively thick stem (about 1cm). The leaves are opposite, oblong to elliptical, with a glossy upper surface. It bears small, pretty, rather unusual flowers **(1)**, about 6cm in length, which are easily missed. They have purple lobes that are twisted at the top, forming a long tube. The sepals are spreading, with hairy margins.
Notes This species is pollinated by small flies.

Ceropegia variegata
APOCYNACEAE FAMILY
3m ◆ perennial

Habitat Dry bushland, usually well hidden within thick bush, where it is protected from browsers, particularly Greater Kudu.
Identification This climber has smooth succulent stems that are green at first, turning greyish later. The leaves **(1)** are scale-like and resemble small hooks along the stem. Flowers are variable in shape and size. The flower tube has two bulges **(2)** at its base and the flower lobes have purple marginal hairs. Small flies pollinate *Ceropegia* species by crawling down the flower tube. Seed pods are borne in pairs, and the seeds are dispersed by the wind.

Desmidorchis acutangula
APOCYNACEAE FAMILY
1m ◆ perennial

Habitat *Acacia-Commiphora* bushland and desert.
Identification A large succulent. The greyish-green stems are thick, angular and four-sided **(1)**. Deep purple flowers, each about 1.5cm in diamater, are clustered together in a rounded inflorescence at the top of a fleshy stem. The seed pods are 10cm or more in length and resemble a pair of horns.

Notes Although they smell unpleasant to humans, the flowers attract flies, which are the main pollinators of this plant.

Desmidorchis foetida
APOCYNACEAE FAMILY
50cm ◆ perennial

Habitat *Acacia* bushland and semi-arid areas.
Identification A succulent herb, similar to *D. speciosa*, but the fleshy, greenish-grey stems are smaller, up to 4cm thick. The flowers are 1.3cm in diameter and the petals have a spotted, warty surface and purple marginal hairs **(1)**. There are purple spots inside the yellowish flowers. The seed pods are 10cm long, nearly cylindrical, with a narrow tip. They are usually in pairs.

Notes Young stems may be peeled and eaten. Although they taste bitter, they can be a temporary source of moisture when no water is available.

Desmidorchis speciosa
APOCYNACEAE FAMILY
80cm ◆ perennial

Habitat Dry, rocky areas in
Acacia bushland.
Identification A succulent plant with
greyish-green stems that are shorter
than those of *D. acutangula*. A few large,
bell-shaped flowers, about 3–5cm
across, are borne in clusters. They have
a yellow interior, dark outer lobes **(1)**,
and purple spotting on the outer edge
of the flower tube **(2)**. Seed pods of
up to 18cm are borne in pairs, and the
seeds are distributed by the wind.

Echidnopsis sharpei
APOCYNACEAE FAMILY
5cm ◆ perennial

Habitat Rocky ground in dry
bushland, or among vegetation that
protects it from being eaten by goats
and other mammals.
Identification A creeping succulent
with rounded stems up to 3cm in
diameter, which are covered in blunt
scale-like leaves **(1)**. Flowers (2cm
across) are borne on very short stalks
and may be dark purple with a yellow
centre, or pale yellow with a purple
centre. The petals are broad at the
base and narrow towards the tip.

Edithcolea grandis
APOCYNACEAE FAMILY
5cm ◆ perennial

Habitat Rocky *Acacia-Commiphora* bushland and, less frequently, dense *Acacia* bushland.
Identification A trailing succulent with sharp knobs along the short, rounded stems. In the shade the stems are green, but when exposed to the sun they turn golden brown. This plant bears possibly the most eye-catching flowers of any stapeliad: several buds form along the top of the main stem, each opening into a large, reddish-brown, rounded flower with five petals edged with purple hairs. The seed pods (1) are pale greyish-green and ribbed.

Huernia keniensis
APOCYNACEAE FAMILY
6cm ◆ perennial

Habitat Semi-arid *Acacia-Commiphora* bushland. Often in rocky crevices or thick bush.
Identification A compact plant with short, succulent stems that have small, fleshy projections (1) scattered along their length. The flowers (2) are variable, but generally bell-shaped, cream on the outside, deep purplish with raised bumps on the inside and up to 2cm across. They have a subtle unpleasant odour and are pollinated mainly by flies. The seed pods appear in pairs and break open when dry to release the seeds, which have silky plumes to enable wind dispersal.

Monolluma socotrana
(Caralluma socotrana)
APOCYNACEAE FAMILY
40cm ◆ perennial

Habitat Dry *Acacia-Commiphora* bushland, at low altitude.
Identification This widespread succulent herb is seldom noticed, except during flowering, when it is a magnificent sight. Many stems of about 1cm diameter branch from the base. These are pale brown or green when in the shade and creamish in full sun. There are visible scars (**1**) where previous years' flowers were attached to the stems. The flowers are bright red with five petals. The twin pods release seeds with tufts of silky hair that aid in wind dispersal.
Notes The flowers have a carrion-like smell and are pollinated mainly by flies. These very attractive succulents do not transplant well and are best left in the wild.

Orbea tubiformis
APOCYNACEAE FAMILY
8cm ◆ perennial

Habitat Dry rocky areas in *Acacia* bushland at moderate altitude.
Identification An upright succulent. The mottled stems are up to 2cm thick and covered with soft, pointed lobes, each about 0.9cm long. Bears solitary, dark purple-brown, cupped flowers with white hairs on the inner surface.

Echinops amplexicaulis
ASTERACEAE FAMILY
1m ◆ perennial

Habitat Open upland grassland.
Identification A prickly, thistle-like plant with broad, stalkless, lobed leaves, each lobe ending in a sharp spike. The stems are slightly ribbed. Numerous crimson flowers are clustered together in a rounded head measuring about 6cm across.
Notes The main taproot is long and thick. Traditionally, the Pokot people prepare it and mix it with milk, then give it to newborns, believing that it helps to prepare the baby's stomach for its mother's milk.

Kleinia abyssinica (Notonia abyssinica)
ASTERACEAE FAMILY
35cm ◆ perennial

Habitat Favours rocky situations and thick protective bush in most habitats, other than desert.
Identification This widespread herb is fleshy and hairless. The leaves are broadly ovate with a narrower tip and entire margins. They often have purple mottling, especially when growing in the shade. Several buds are borne at the top of stems; usually opening one at a time, revealing a reddish-orange flowerhead.

Kleinia gregorii
(Notonia gregorii)
ASTERACEAE FAMILY
18cm ◆ perennial

Habitat Open grassland and rocky
positions in dry *Acacia* bushland.
Identification When not flowering,
this upright succulent is easy to miss
among the grasses. Fleshy, variegated
stems up to 1cm thick branch from
the base. They lack leaves entirely. The
bright red flowers are borne at the
tips of thin flowering stems that arise
from the tops of the succulent stems.
Several flowers may be carried on the
same plant, but it does not flower as
prolifically as other *Kleinia* species.

Stictocardia macalusoi
CONVOLVULACEAE FAMILY
10m ◆ perennial

Habitat Moist forest along the coast.
Identification This is a very robust
liana, with broad, well-veined,
heart-shaped leaves up to 7cm long,
and trumpet-shaped blooms that
are bright scarlet with a paler or
yellowish inner tube.
Notes A member of the morning
glory family, it is much loved by
gardeners, but should be planted
with caution,
as it can be a
tenacious climber.

Euphorbia cryptospinosa
EUPHORBIACEAE FAMILY
80cm ◆ perennial

Habitat Dry grassland and *Acacia-Commiphora* bushland.
Identification This tall, upright *Euphorbia* is so well camouflaged in its habitat, especially in grassy areas, that is very easily overlooked. It has soft ridges **(1)** on the surface of the stems and very tiny spines, less than 3mm long. Small reddish-purple flowers **(2)**, up to 0.6cm across, lie almost flat against the stems.
Notes The name *cryptospinosa* means 'hidden spines'.

Euphorbia heterospina ssp. *baringoensis*
EUPHORBIACEAE FAMILY
5m ◆ perennial

Habitat Dry *Acacia* bushland.
Identification A tall, upright shrub that may exceed its average height of 5m if supported. Paired grey prickles **(1)** run along the angled margins of the stems, at intervals of about 2cm, and the brick-red flowers **(2)** grow along these margins too. They are oppositely arranged and alternate with the prickles. When dry, the three-sided seed pods pop to disperse seeds over a wide area.

Notes Kudus and baboons feed on the stems, and doves eat the seeds. The flowers provide nectar for flies, beetles, ants and bees. Honey from the nectar of this plant is a traditional treatment for coughs and colds.

Gladiolus watsonioides
IRIDACEAE FAMILY
1m ◆ perennial

Habitat Montane moorland and open grassland. Favours shallow, damp soils and rocky ground; often grows among heather or near streams.

Identification An upright lily that arises from a corm. The stems are smooth and hairless, with 5–7 sword-shaped leaves. The leaves higher up on the stem are shorter than lower ones. A nodding flower spike holds 12 or more alternately arranged flowers. Each is entirely red, measures 8–10cm in length and has a downward-curving tube.

Agelanthus oehleri (Tapinanthus oehleri)
LORANTHACEAE FAMILY
80cm ◆ perennial

Habitat The margins of dry cedar-olive forest; also occurs in other semi-arid environments.

Identification This attractive parasitic shrub is widespread and fairly conspicuous in suitable habitat, where it grows on many different tree and shrub species. The obovate, slightly fleshy leaves (1) are alternately arranged along short, smooth stems. Upright flowers with a bulbous base (2) emerge from the leaf axils. The thin red flower tube is ridged and up to 4cm long, with a yellow band near the top and a purple tip. The fruits have a warty surface.

Hibiscus aponeurus
MALVACEAE FAMILY
2m ◆ perennial

Habitat Dry, open grassland.
Identification A tall, upright plant or small shrub with rough stems covered in close hairs. The leaves are ovate with serrated margins **(1)** and are densely covered in tiny star-shaped hairs. Solitary bright red or pink flowers are borne on short stalks emerging from the leaf axils.
Notes May occur together with *H. flavifolius* although it is not as widespread.

Striga asiatica
OROBANCHACEAE FAMILY
30cm ◆ perennial

Habitat Among various host grasses, including agricultural crops such as maize, on dry, nutrient-poor soils in coastal, inland and upland environments. Widespread.
Identification This upright, semi-parasitic herb has hairy stems and narrow, lanceolate leaves that are also clothed in soft hairs. It bears loose spikes of conspicuous, very bright flowers. The pods are small and contain tiny seeds that are dispersed by wind or water. The seeds germinate and attach themselves directly to the roots of a host plant, from which they feed and on which they depend for their survival.
Notes This plant can be a serious pest of cereal crops and is considered an invasive alien, particularly where it has been introduced beyond its natural range.

Rumex usambarensis
POLYGONACEAE FAMILY
2m ◆ perennial

Habitat Along the margins of moist forest at higher altitude.
Identification A scrambling climber or shrub with clustered leaves that are linear, but with a triangular base. Small red or reddish-brown flowers with large sepals are loosely arranged in a branching inflorescence (panicle).
Notes This is one of several 'wild rhubarb' species: when peeled, the stems, which have a sour taste, can be chewed as a snack.

Pentas parvifolia
RUBIACEAE FAMILY
2m ◆ perennial

Habitat Forest margins at higher altitude; some relict plants survive in rocky areas at moderate altitude, where they were once abundant.
Identification A straggly shrub, most parts of which are hairy. The leaves are opposite and lanceolate, with small stipules at their base **(1)**. The showy, scarlet flowers (about 1.4cm in length) are carried in bunches at the tops of branches.

Hypoestes aristata
ACANTHACEAE FAMILY
2m ◆ perennial

Habitat In thickets within *Acacia* bushland and on the margins of moist upland forest.
Identification A fairly bushy herb. Small appressed hairs cover the stems, and showy flowers are carried in bunches just above the leaves, which are broadest at the base with a narrow tip. The upper lip of each flower is marked with small pink spots.
Notes This is an attractive garden plant, whose flowers attract sunbirds.

Hypoestes forskaolii
ACANTHACEAE FAMILY
40cm ◆ perennial

Habitat There are two varieties of *H. forskaolii* – the less hairy species shown here tends to be found at moderate to higher altitude; the other variety occurs in hot, arid areas in *Acacia-Commiphora* bushland.
Identification This is a small, well-branched, clump-forming herb. The leaves are dark green and elliptical, with a covering of somewhat apressed hairs. Bunches of purple or pale pink flowers are borne in the leaf axils along the stems. The top petal of each flower has three small lobes that curve backward, and there are glandular hairs on the sepals.
Notes The blossoms are much loved by bees and butterflies.

Justicia betonica
ACANTHACEAE FAMILY
30cm ◆ perennial

Habitat Occurs mainly in semi-arid bushland.
Identification This upright herb has smooth, elliptical leaves with slightly wavy margins. The flowers are carried on a spike covered in leafy bracts (**1**), which are largely translucent, with a slight pattern of green netting. The flowers are two-lipped, ageing from white through pink to violet.

Justicia bracteata
ACANTHACEAE FAMILY
20cm ◆ perennial

Habitat Dry *Acacia* bushland and the margins of dry cedar-olive forest.
Identification A rather hairy herb with broadly lanceolate leaves. The flowering stems, up to 5cm long, have distinctive leafy bracts; flowers are purplish-pink. Seeds are borne in small woody capsules.
Notes When peeled, the softly hairy stems release a pleasant vanilla-like scent, which has been used as a perfume in some traditional communities.

Justicia diclipteroides
ACANTHACEAE FAMILY
40cm ◆ **perennial**

Habitat *Acacia* bushland and open grassland.
Identification A small herb with softly hairy stems, broad-based leaves up to 4cm long, and eye-catching purple-red flowers, 8–10cm long, which are spread out along the stems. The sepals are about 0.7cm long.
Notes This pretty herb brightens up the dry bush at times when there are no other flowers. Small stingless bees collect the pollen.

Thunbergia holstii
ACANTHACEAE FAMILY
2m ◆ **perennial**

Habitat *Acacia* and *Acacia-Commiphora* bushland, often on rocky hills. Also in coastal bushland. Occurs from near sea level to about 1,700m.
Identification A woody shrub with angled stems and smooth, shiny, elliptical leaves with wavy margins. It bears conspicuous tubular flowers, 5cm in length, and comprising five petals. Flowers are purple with a bright yellow throat.

Achyranthus aspera
AMARANTHACEAE FAMILY
3m ◆ perennial

Habitat Disturbed ground, often in shaded areas in *Acacia* bushland; also found in fallow fields on arable land.
Identification A widespread, straggly herb that often scrambles up into other vegetation. It has softly hairy stems and rounded to lanceolate leaves. The flowers, borne on a long raceme, are pale pink, turning darker once pollinated. The sepals, which are spiny to aid in seed dispersal, often catch on clothing and pierce the skin.
Notes Young leaves may be cooked like spinach or eaten raw as a salad.

Digera muricata
AMARANTHACEAE FAMILY
70cm ◆ annual

Habitat Dry *Acacia-Commiphora* bushland and open grassland.
Identification This tall herb has few branches. Its leaves are narrow and ovate, 5–6cm long, with entire margins and a pointed tip. The pale pink flowers are borne on leaning racemes.
Notes Bushland areas take on an attractive pink hue after the rains, when *D. muricata* is in full flower.

Ammocharis tinneana
AMARYLLIDACEAE FAMILY
15cm ◆ **perennial**

Habitat Shallow soils in flat, open *Acacia* bushland. Tolerates both sunny and semi-shaded positions.
Identification This locally common plant arises from a large underground bulb that is dormant until just before the rains, when the leaves emerge, spreading out on the ground in two fan-like arrays to form a basal rosette. They are followed by up to 20 flowers carried on a short, thick stalk, which emerges from beneath the leaves. The petals curl backwards and are pale pink at first, turning darker once pollinated. The reddish fruits drop to the ground when ripe.

Adenium obesum
APOCYNACEAE FAMILY
6m ◆ **perennial**

Habitat Dry, coastal *Brachystegia* woodland; also semi-arid country to the north and lava soils in the Rift Valley. Plants at the coast tend to be more squat.
Identification An attractive succulent with an inflated caudex (trunk). Highly variable, it may be small and squat or over 6m. Smooth grey (or golden, in northern Kenya) branches arise from its base. The leaves, which are elliptical or rounded, smooth or hairy, depending on the variety, are carried in rosettes at the tips of branches. There are both pink and white-flowered varieties, although the white is uncommon. Silky hairs on the seeds aid in wind dispersal.
Notes Traditionally, hunter gatherers would boil the roots and dip their arrowheads in the poisonous, viscous paste produced.

Ceropegia denticulata
APOCYNACEAE FAMILY
3m ◆ perennial

Habitat Dry *Acacia* bushland, where it usually occurs in thick bush.
Identification This succulent climber has squarish green stems and fleshy, ovate leaves. The upright flowers consist of a pale tube, 4cm long, and petal lobes with green, white and dark purple stripes. The petals are covered with purple hairs **(1)**. The seed pods resemble two thin horns. Once dry, they split open, releasing the seeds, which have silky plumes that aid wind dispersal.

Aloe myriacantha
ASPHODELACEAE FAMILY
20cm ◆ perennial

Habitat Open grassland; often forms pure stands.
Identification East Africa's smallest aloe, *A. myriacantha* is also known as the grass aloe. It is easy to miss among the grasses, except when it bears its flowers or fruit. The leaves, 10–12cm x 1cm, have toothed margins and white flecks at the base. They form a basal rosette that protects a single flowering stem, 20cm tall, which carries a head of drooping, pinkish-red flowers. The buds are upright, with a slightly curved tip. A dry fruit capsule encloses the winged seeds.

Aloe scabrifolia

ASPHODELACEAE FAMILY
1m ◆ perennial

Habitat Hot, dry *Acacia-Commiphora* bushland.
Identification An *Aloe* that branches at its base, producing stems that sprawl along the ground. A rosette of leaves arises at the tip of each stem, and these rosettes may eventually form large clumps. The leaves are greyish and thick, with a rough texture. Dull, pinkish-red lowers are borne on the branches of a flowering stem up to 1m tall. They are 'secund', i.e. arranged alternately along just one side of the branch.

Carduus keniensis

ASTERACEAE FAMILY
2m ◆ perennial

Habitat Open grassland at high altitude.
Identification This plant forms a thick rosette (1) of spiny, pinnate, greenish-grey leaves. The many pinkish-mauve florets, which are borne on very short stems, are crowded at the tip of the central stem.

149

Carduus nyassanus subsp. *kikuyorum*

ASTERACEAE FAMILY

2m ◆ perennial

Habitat Moist montane forest.
Identification A fairly tall plant. The leaves are dark green, pinnate and elliptical, with soft marginal spines (1) up to 1cm long. The leaf surface is covered in glandular hairs. Pale mauve flowers are borne in heads that emerge from the leaf axils or from the tips of stems.
Notes Bees collect nectar from the flowers.

Carduus schimperi *(C. chamaecephalus)*

ASTERACEAE FAMILY

3.5cm ◆ perennial

Habitat Open grassland at high altitude; extends into the Alpine zone.
Identification This spiny plant is common in its range and bears a rosette of leaves that lie close to the ground and are lobed and spiny with a purple rachis (1). The pinkish-mauve flowers arise, four to five at a time, from the centre of the rosette.
Notes The thistle-like flowers are well loved by bees, which collect the nectar.

Gutenbergia cordifolia
ASTERACEAE FAMILY
20cm ◆ annual

Habitat Dry open grassland and disturbed ground.
Identification A small, locally common herb with lanceolate, nearly stalkless leaves that have a white, felt-like undersurface. The purple flowers, commonly known as 'pope's buttons', are compact, rounded and arranged at the tips of stems. The bracts are covered in soft, woolly white hairs.
Notes Blister beetles seem to enjoy feeding on the petals. This is also an important fodder plant for cattle in semi-arid areas.

Helichrysum formossisimum
ASTERACEAE FAMILY
2m ◆ perennial

Habitat Moorland, where it is abundant among tussock grasses and along the edges of the bamboo zone.
Identification An important moorland species, this tall plant has finely hairy, woolly-looking leaves, which are ovate to lanceolate and 2–10cm long. It bears pink or white flowers.

Kleinia squarrosa
ASTERACEAE FAMILY
3m ◆ **perennial**

Habitat Dry *Acacia* bushland.
Identification A robust shrub with
smooth, rounded stems marked
with thin purple stripes. The leaves
are ovate and hairless, with a subtle
purple tinge on the margins. The
flowers, which are pink to mauve,
or sometimes purple, are borne in
bunches at the tips of stems.
Notes Many
insects frequent
the flowers,
especially
butterflies, the
main pollinators
of this species.

Senecio roseiflorus
ASTERACEAE FAMILY
1m ◆ **perennial**

Habitat Rocky ground and moorland
on lower mountain slopes.
Identification A tall and shrubby
plant that is covered in sticky glands.
The leaves
are lanceolate and hairy,
with margins that
curl slightly under.
Bunches of flowers
in various shades
of purple appear
together at the tips
of branches. The
sepals are clothed in
soft hairs.

Sphaeranthus ukambensis
ASTERACEAE FAMILY
1m ◆ perennial

Habitat Clayey soils in flooded open grassland and some drier habitats.
Identification A tall herb with rough, hairy, winged stems and softly hairy, slightly folded, lanceolate leaves that have wavy, toothed margins. The flowers – purple, pink or mauve – are cylindrical and up to 2cm long.
Notes This is one of the most commonly encountered *Sphaeranthus* species. Its pleasant smell is characteristic of many damp habitats in its range.

Vernonia brachycalyx
ASTERACEAE FAMILY
2m ◆ perennial

Habitat Common on forest margins at moderate altitude; often associated with cedar-olive forest.
Identification A climbing herb or shrub with thin stems. The leaves are broad, slightly folded, toothed or entire, with woolly hairs on the undersurface. Pretty flowers are carried in bunches at the tips of flowering stalks, and can be purple, mauve or almost white.
Notes This species makes an attractive garden plant and is well loved by butterflies.

Vernonia cinerascens
ASTERACEAE FAMILY
80cm ◆ perennial

Habitat Dry *Acacia-Commiphora* bushland; appears to favour sandy soils.
Identification An upright herb with woolly stems and bunches of small, obovate leaves, 3–4cm long, with a rounded apex **(1)**. The deep purple to mauve flowers are spread out on terminal branches and, from a distance, are often less noticeable than the whitish seeds.

Vernonia lasiopus
ASTERACEAE FAMILY
1.5m ◆ perennial

Habitat The margins of moist upland forest and in nearby areas of cultivation.
Identification A shrubby plant with hairy, ovate leaves, up to 6cm long, with coarsely toothed margins. Pale purple bunches of flowers are borne at the tips of branches, and the stamens are exserted.
Notes This is an important food plant for many species, especially butterflies, flies and bees.

Impatiens pseudoviola
BALSAMINACEAE FAMILY
12cm ◆ annual

Habitat Moist upland forest.
Identification This abundant, short-lived annual has shiny, nearly heart-shaped leaves with small hairs along their margins. The stems take root if they touch the ground. The pale pink flowers are 2.5cm in diameter and there are two yellow spots at the base of each lateral petal.

Impatiens sodenii
BALSAMINACEAE FAMILY
1m ◆ perennial

Habitat Fairly widespread at altitudes between 1,000 and 2,500m. It occurs close to waterfalls, where it can benefit from the mist or spray.
Identification A tall, bushy herb that branches from the base. The stems are succulent and green, and the leaves are elliptical with a pointed apex and stiff purple hairs along the margins **(1)**. It bears large flowers that vary in colour from dark pink to white. The seed pods are green.

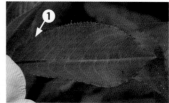

Begonia johnstonii
BEGONIACEAE FAMILY
20cm ◆ perennial

Habitat The margins of streams
and rivers in moist upland forest at
moderate to high altitude.
Identification An uncommon,
upright *Begonia* with fleshy stems.
The leaves are asymmetrical, with
bluntly toothed margins and a
reddish undersurface (1). It bears
pink flowers of about 3cm in
diameter, followed by winged fruits.

Cyphia glandulifera
CAMPANULACEAE FAMILY
15cm ◆ perennial

Habitat Varies,
but favours
shallow soils in dry
bushed grassland;
also occurs in
upland habitats.
Identification A
widespread, upright
plant, *C. glandulifera*
produces a rosette
of rounded or
narrow leaves, up
to 6cm long, with
small teeth along
their margins.
Pretty little pink
or mauve flowers
alternate along the
stem. The sepals
bend backward.

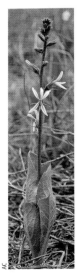

AC

DM

Silene burchellii
CARYOPHYLLACEAE FAMILY
15cm ◆ **perennial**

Habitat Open upland grassland.
Identification An uncommon,
delicate herb with deeply lobed, linear
leaves **(1)**. The flowers have a purple-
striped floral tube, which is softly
hairy, and divided petals. They vary in
colour from pink to white

Silene macrosolen
CARYOPHYLLACEAE FAMILY
30cm ◆ **perennial**

Habitat Waterlogged open grassland
at moderate altitude.
Identification This is an uncommon,
delicate plant that forms a rosette,
similar to, but larger than, that of
S. burchelli. The entire plant is hairless.
Its leaves are smooth and linear, with
a pointed tip. The flowers have a long
floral tube marked with purple stripes;
the petals are pink to almost white,
and the entire inflorescence is covered
in sticky patches.

Cleome allamanii
CLEOMACEAE FAMILY
20cm ◆ annual

Habitat Dry *Acacia-Commiphora*
bushland; often found on bare ground.
Identification This striking dryland
herb emerges after the first rains and
is sticky to the touch, as its leaves
and stems are covered in glandular
hairs. It bears palmate leaves with 5–7
narrow leaflets. The purple flowers
have yellow markings on both upper
petals **(1)**. There are 6–8 stamens.
Glandular hairs also cover the seed
pods, which measure about 6cm.

Cleome hirta
CLEOMACEAE FAMILY
15cm ◆ annual

Habitat Marshy ground in coastal
bushland, where it is locally common
and widespread after the rains.
Also occurs in open grassland and
disturbed areas.
Identification Like *C. allamanii*, this
plant is glandular and sticky to the
touch. Its leaves **(1)** are palmate, with
5–6 broad leaflets, and the flowers are
pale mauve with white markings. The
sepals are covered in small hairs.

Cleome monophylla
CLEOMACEAE FAMILY
23cm ◆ annual

Habitat Open grassland, *Acacia* bushland and pockets of shallow soil over rocky ground.
Identification An upright plant with simple, lanceolate leaves, up to 6cm long, with a broad base, a narrower tip and tiny marginal hairs. The pink flowers are small and delicate, fading after pollination to a paler shade. Glandular hairs cover the seed pods, which are straight and up to 7cm in length.

Murdannia simplex
COMMELINACEAE FAMILY
20cm ◆ perennial

Habitat Open grassland and swampy grassland areas at moderate altitude.
Identification A delicate herb with a rosette (**1**) of narrow leaves, which are deep purple when growing in sunny positions. The mauve flowers are borne on a long, thin stalk that arises from the rosette. They measure about 2cm across and have one upper and two lateral petals.

Ipomoea cairica
CONVOLVULACEAE FAMILY
3m ◆ perennial

Habitat Riverine vegetation and the margins of dry cedar-olive forest.
Identification An attractive climber with tough, warty stems, palmate leaves with five or more lobes **(1)**, and flowers that vary from purple to white.
Notes This climber has potential as a garden plant to cover a pergola or veranda and provide shade. It has attractive foliage, making it an appealing garden subject even when not in flower.

Ipomoea cicatricosa
CONVOLVULACEAE FAMILY
2.5m ◆ perennial

Habitat Dry *Acacia-Commiphora* bushland.
Identification A rather robust, woody herb or small shrub with knobbly leaf scars on the stems and softly hairy branches. Flowers up to 7cm across are mauve or pale violet with a darker centre. They often appear before the leaves, but can also occur with them, depending on the rains. The leaves are broad and fold slightly inward. A rounded capsule bears the seeds, which are covered in silky golden hairs.
Notes This plant, which often forms pure stands, flowers prolifically, bringing the arid landscape to life.

Ipomoea donaldsonii
CONVOLVULACEAE FAMILY
2m ◆ perennial

Habitat Dry *Acacia-Commiphora* bushland.
Identification An attractive shrub with small, rounded, pale green leaves. The bark **(1)** peels from the trunk and branches in small, yellow scrolls, allowing the new bark beneath to photosynthesise. The flowers are purple or white with a dark centre.
Notes Stingless bees collect the pollen.

Ipomoea ficifolia
CONVOLVULACEAE FAMILY
2.5m ◆ perennial

Habitat Exclusive to coastal bushland.
Identification An attractive climber with bristly hairs on the stems. It often covers areas of bare ground. The leaves may be entire or lobed **(1)**, and the flowers are up to 5cm long. There are glandular hairs on the sepals.

Ipomoea hildebrandtii
CONVOLVULACEAE FAMILY
2.5m ◆ perennial

Habitat Open ground in drier *Acacia* bushland areas; often seen along roadsides and in ditches.
Identification A compact herb that branches from its base. The broad leaves **(1)** are often folded and have soft hairs on the undersurface. This very pretty *Ipomoea* bears pale pink or pinkish-purple flowers.

Ipomoea jaegerii
CONVOLVULACEAE FAMILY
20cm ◆ perennial

Habitat Rocky hillsides at moderate altitude, where it grows among grasses, or in open areas with shallow soils.
Identification This low, spreading, very leafy herb has narrow leaves that fold slightly inwards. Abundant flowers, measuring about 10cm across, usually emerge with the leaves. The seeds are clothed in golden hairs.
Notes Small stingless bees and honey bees depend heavily on *Ipomoea* flowers for pollen.

Ipomoea kituiensis
CONVOLVULACEAE FAMILY
5m ◆ perennial

Habitat Associated with *Rhus* and *Carissa* species in *Acacia* bushland at higher altitude; also along the edges of dry cedar-olive forest. Tolerates various soils, from lateritic to granitic.
Identification A robust shrub or climber that may even exceed 5m with support. The undersides of the rounded leaves are covered in soft white hairs. Flowers are borne in bunches, and are pale purple to almost white, with a darker centre. The sepals are narrow and thread-like.
Notes Maasai herbalists use the roots as a traditional treatment to arrest bleeding and miscarriage in early pregnancy.

Ipomoea oenotherae
CONVOLVULACEAE FAMILY
4cm ◆ perennial

Habitat Shallow soils over rocky ground in *Acacia* bushland or in open grassland.
Identification A small herb that emerges after good seasonal rains. The leaves may be simple or have up to eight lobes. The flowers, measuring 3cm in diamater, vary in colour from purple to white or yellow.
Notes The edible, tuberous roots (1) are enjoyed by pastoralist children when they are out herding livestock.

Ipomoea pes-tigridis
CONVOLVULACEAE FAMILY
3m ◆ annual

Habitat Confined to coastal bushland and adjacent coastal belt vegetation.
Identification This climber has hairy, trailing stems. It may scramble up into nearby vegetation or spread out on the ground. Its leaves are palmate, with up to eight narrow lobes. It flowers sparsely, producing stalkless blooms that measure up to 5cm in length. They are pale purple, pink or white and have a dark throat.

Pterocephalus frutescens (Cephalaria pungens)
DIPSACACEAE FAMILY
20cm ◆ perennial

Habitat Open montane grassland.
Identification An upright herb with irregularly toothed, lanceolate leaves, which are softly hairy on both surfaces. It carries globular flower heads that range from deep pink to pale mauve, comprising tube-shaped flowers with protruding anthers. The fruits are ball-shaped and covered in long, soft hairs.

Scabiosa columbaria
DIPSACACEAE FAMILY
15cm ◆ perennial

Habitat Open grassland and rocky slopes at higher altitude; favours shallow soils.
Identification A small herb with a rosette of divided leaves, up to 10cm long, at its base. Solitary pink or mauve flower heads 3.5cm in diameter are borne on 8cm-long flowering stalks. The sepals enclosing the fruits are covered in long hairs **(1)**.

Sansevieria suffruticosa
DRACAENACEA FAMILY
40cm ◆ perennial

Habitat Dry rocky ground, usually in a semi-shaded position in bushland.
Identification An attractive succulent with spreading, faintly variegated leaves, which are somewhat rounded in cross-section. It is rhizomatous, and plants will spread to cover a large area if left undisturbed. The flowers may be pale pink to white.

Erica whyteana
ERICACEAE FAMILY
50cm ◆ perennial

Habitat Marshes and the margins of streams at high altitude.
Identification This tough little shrub is one of the smaller Ericaceae. It has tiny, needle-like leaves, which are carried close to the stem. The inflorescence (1) is a spike bearing bell-shaped flowers ranging from deep magenta or pink to white.

Euphorbia neostapelioides
(Monadenium stapelioides)
EUPHORBIACEAE FAMILY
10cm ◆ perennial

Habitat Open grassland and shallow soils overlying rocky ground.
Identification This succulent trailing herb has fairly thick stems that arise from a tuberous rootstock and bear conspicuous leaf scars (1). The leaves vary from narrow to broad and tend to be green with purple markings when the plant is situated in a shaded position, but purplish with deeper purple markings in sunny locations. The flowers are carried on short, thick stems at the tips of branches, and the seeds are enclosed in a three-sided capsule.

Lysimachia serpens (Anagallis serpens)

GENTIANACEAE FAMILY

2.5cm ◆ annual/perennial

Habitat Alpine marshes and the margins of mountain streams. Requires an open, sunny or semi-shaded position. **Identification** A trailing plant that creeps along the ground forming carpets of slightly fleshy, oval, alternating leaves. The stems root at the nodes. It bears small flowers with petals up to 1cm long, which have prominent veins. It is a variable species: in some cases the leaves are crowded and overlap, in others they are upright. The flower petals average 0.5cm in some plants and 1cm in others.

Geranium ocellatum

GERANIACEAE FAMILY

12cm ◆ annual

Habitat Open and deeply shaded situations in bushed grassland at moderate to high altitude. Moisture-loving, it is generally found after good rains and disappears quite quickly once the bush starts to dry out. **Identification** A delicate herb that spreads over a wide area. It has many short branches bearing softly hairy, deeply lobed leaves with toothed margins. The purple-pink flowers have black centres and appear in pairs. The seeds are ridged at the base and are dark brown when ripe.

Monsonia senegalensis
GERANIACEAE FAMILY
10cm ◆ annual

Habitat Sandy, granitic soils in dry
Acacia bushland and open grassland.
Identification A small annual that
branches from its base and has several
hairy stems. The leaves, which are
carried on stalks of up to 5cm, have
a broad base, toothed margins and
obvious leaf veins on the upper
surface. The flowers are small and
solitary, up to 1.2cm long. The petals
are pale pink with darker veins. The
fruit is long, up to 1cm.

Ledebouria kirkii (Scilla kirkii)
HYACINTHACEAE FAMILY
20cm ◆ perennial

Habitat At moderate altitude in dry
Acacia-Commiphora bushland; also
associated with *Rhus* and *Carissa*
species in rocky bushland.
Identification This attractive dryland
plant has a large underground bulb
and comes up with the rains, sending
out its leaves first. These are broad
and shiny green, with dark purple
blotches. Many flowers are alternately
arranged along the 15–20cm-long
flowering stalk. The pale green petals
bend all the way backward to expose a
bright purple-pink centre.

Dierama cupuliflorum
IRIDACEAE FAMILY
1m ◆ perennial

Habitat Moorland and open marshy grassland at higher altitude.
Identification A tall iris that arises from a rhizomatous rootstock. It has long, flattened, linear leaves, and a long flowering stalk with tubular flowers that are pale pink to reddish purple, and hang from the main stem on delicate stalks. Small groups are usually found growing close together.
Notes This would be a rewarding plant for a high-altitude garden.

Aeollanthus densiflorus (A. stormsii)
LAMIACEAE FAMILY
40cm ◆ perennial

Habitat Shallow soil on exposed rocky hills and mountains. Often associated with dry cedar-olive forests.
Identification Less common than its relative *A. repens*, this shrubby herb has rounded, softly hairy leaves with toothed margins. The pinkish-mauve flowers are usually quite pale and are densely arranged on a short spike, which may be up to 6cm long. The upper petals are marked with purple spots and lines.

Aeollanthus repens
LAMIACEAE FAMILY
30cm ◆ perennial

Habitat Rocky areas with shallow soil in *Acacia* bushland.
Identification A compact succulent herb with softly hairy, toothed leaves. Flowering stems up to 30cm emerge from a base of fleshy leaves. Flowers may be various shades of purple or mauve and are sometimes very pale. The flower bract has a dark purple gland (**1**).

Clinopodium abyssinicum
LAMIACEAE FAMILY
40cm ◆ perennial

Habitat Grassland and rocky bushland at higher altitude.
Identification This delicate herb has many branches covered in ovate leaves up to 2cm long, with serrated margins. The leaves give off a strong peppermint-like smell when crushed. Small, rose-pink flowers are carried on an inflorescence of 6 or 7cm. The lower lip of each flower has three lobes with small purple spots. The sepals are slightly ridged (**1**).
Notes The leaves can be used to make a pleasant-tasting herbal infusion.

Micromeria imbricata
(Satureia biflora)
LAMIACEAE FAMILY
50cm ◆ **perennial**

Habitat Open upland grassland.
Identification A rather woody herb
with many short, compact leaves in an
opposite arrangement along the stems.
The leaves have a hairy undersurface
and pale margins. Small, leaf-like bracts
hold the tiny flowers, which are pink,
violet or white, and are concentrated
towards the tops of the stems.

Ocimum spectabile
LAMIACEAE FAMILY
2m ◆ **perennial**

Habitat Dry *Acacia-
Commiphora* bushland.
Identification A big, bushy shrub
with squarish stems and broadly
elliptical leaves with toothed margins.
The inflorescence is a hairy raceme
of woolly-looking, pale purple
flowers **(1)**. The sepal tube is covered
in long, branched hairs.
Notes This shrub is a lovely sight when
in full flower in dry bushland. It is also
an important food plant for bees.

Orthosiphon parvifolius
LAMIACEAE FAMILY
15cm ◆ perennial

Habitat Locally common in black cotton or shallow soils and in open flooded grassland.
Identification A small, compact herb with many squarish, softly hairy stems branching from the base. The greyish, ovate leaves have serrated margins, an opposite arrangement and fold slightly inward. Bunches of five or six pale pink flowers are spaced out along the raceme. The sepals are purplish.

Lindernia serpens
LINDERNIACEAE FAMILY
4cm ◆ perennial

Habitat Rocky situations with very shallow soils in *Acacia* bushland.
Identification This tiny plant has smooth, narrow, alternate leaves, which are hairless and up to 1cm in length. Small flowers emerge from the leaf axils on stalks **(1)** up to 1cm long. They have three lower petals and one upper lip and can be pink, pale mauve or lilac, with a white throat.

MWS

Abutilon longicuspe
MALVACEAE FAMILY
2m ◆ **perennial**

Habitat The margins of dry cedar-olive forest and open grassland at higher altitude.
Identification A tall, straggly shrub with glandular hairs along the stems **(1)**. The leaves are heart-shaped and softly hairy. Numerous purplish flowers, up to 2.5cm in diameter, are borne at the tips of loosely hanging stems.
Notes The leaves and flowers of all Malvaceae are edible.

Hermannia kirkii
MALVACEAE FAMILY
25cm ◆ **annual**

Habitat Dry *Acacia-Commiphora* bushland.
Identification This uncommon annual is delicate, with thin branches, and the entire plant is covered with glandular hairs. The leaves are narrow, with serrated margins, but with a broad base, and the pendent flowers emerge from the leaf axils. Seeds are carried in a capsule measuring about 0.2cm.

Hibiscus meyeri
MALVACEAE FAMILY
2m ◆ perennial

Habitat Dry *Acacia* bushland. Also
occurs along the coastal belt.
Identification A widespread, variable
Hibiscus with tall, upright stems
and ovate, slightly hairy leaves. The
flowers vary from pale pink to whitish,
depending on where the plant is
found. Both stems and leaves are
covered in tiny star-shaped hairs.
Notes The Pokot people use the
stems to manufacture woven
partitions for their homes.

Pavonia urens
MALVACEAE FAMILY
3m ◆ perennial

Habitat The margins of dry cedar-
olive forest and open clearings in
moist upland forest.
Identification A widespread, tall,
shrub-like plant that is generally hairy.
The leaves are round with up to seven
triangular lobes, and the flowers may be
solitary or clustered at the tips of stems.
Notes A useful source of fodder for
livestock, especially sheep and goats.
The flowers can be eaten raw or cooked.

Boerhavia helenae
(Commicarpus helenae)
NYCTAGINACEAE FAMILY
15cm ◆ perennial

Habitat *Acacia-Commiphora* bushland.
Identification This trailing herb is fairly common in suitable habitat. It has pale stems and light green, broadly ovate leaves with slightly wavy margins. Flowering stems up to 4cm long emerge from the leaf axils. Bunches of up to 12 small pink, mauve or purple flowers are borne at the tips of these stems. The sepals measure about 0.7cm.

Boerhavia pedunculusa
(Commicarpus pedunculosus)
NYCTAGINACEAE FAMILY
10cm ◆ perennial

Habitat Dry *Acacia* bushland and rocky open grassland.
Identification A trailing herb with broad, smooth, hairless leaves. The flowering stalk is quite long (about 10cm) and carries a simple arrangement of magenta-pink flowers at its tip. The fruits are sticky to the touch.

Epilobium stereophyllum
ONAGRACEAE FAMILY
30cm ✦ perennial

Habitat Open upland grassland; usually found among grasses close to streams or rivers.

Identification This plant produces running stems (stolons) along the ground, which root at the nodes. The leaves are stalkless, lanceolate and faintly toothed, and the pink or mauve flowers are carried at the tips of long stalks. The pink to mauve petals are up to 1.2cm and notched. Small, soft hairs cover the leaves and stems.

Disa stairsii
ORCHIDACEAE FAMILY
1m ✦ perennial

Habitat Moist high-altitude forest, moorland and swampland; favours volcanic soils.

Identification This tall, slender ground orchid has a tuberous root system. A rosette of leaves at its base produces a cylindrical flowering spike, densely covered with bright pink flowers 0.2–0.3cm across, each with a distinctive, pendulous middle sepal. In flower, *D. stairsii* is a very striking plant.

Eulophia cucullata
ORCHIDACEAE FAMILY
1m ◆ perennial

Habitat Open glades in moist forest; also in open grassland.
Identification A ground orchid with a tall flowering spike that bears a bright, showy raceme of approximately 3–8 flowers, each with three broad, pale to deep pink petals, the lower one curved to form a tube, with a touch of yellow at its throat and two horn-like appendages **(1)**. The broad-based sepals bend far backward. Three or four linear leaves appear after the flowers. The seed pod measures up to 4cm.

Eulophia horsfallii
ORCHIDACEAE FAMILY
2m ◆ perennial

Habitat Wetlands, such as marshes and swamps in moist upland forest.
Identification This tall ground orchid has folded leaves that may reach 1m in length. The flowers are clustered together on an inflorescence 1–2m tall. The upper petals hang down over the lower petal, which has three yellow-tinged ridges, and the sepals are recurved. The seed pods have a slightly ridged surface and measure up to 5cm when mature.

Satyrium crassicaule
ORCHIDACEAE FAMILY
1m ◆ perennial

Habitat Damp, swampy locations in open upland grassland.
Identification A tall orchid with lanceolate leaves held close to the stem. The flowers are crowded on a flowering spike measuring about 4cm, borne at the tip of the stem. This orchid tends to form clumps and is most attractive when in flower. The flowers can be various shades of purple. The sepals face upright.

Cycnium cameronianum
OROBANCHACEAE FAMILY
25cm ◆ annual

Habitat Dry *Acacia-Commiphora* bushland.
Identification A tall plant with hairy stems and leaves up to 6cm long. The lower leaves are more deeply toothed than those higher up. The flowers are pink with a darker centre, and are alternately arranged along an erect, 20cm-tall raceme.

Ghikaea speciosa
OROBANCHACEAE FAMILY
2m ◆ **perennial**

Habitat Confined to *Acacia-Commiphora* bushland.
Identification A tall, erect, bushy shrub. The leaves are alternate and oval, and the stems are slightly hairy. The flowers may be mauve to pink and are crowded in bunches at the tips of stems.

Oxalis latifolia
OXALIDACEAE FAMILY
8cm ◆ **annual**

Habitat Cultivated fields and gardens at higher altitude.
Identification A small herb with no stems: the leaf petioles and flowering stalks emerge directly from an underground bulb. Roughly heart-shaped leaves are arranged in groups of three. The inflorescence comprises up to eight purple flowers with pale green, yellow-tipped sepals **(1)**.
Notes It has edible, tart-tasting leaves.

Canavalia cathartica
PAPILIONACEAE FAMILY
3m ◆ perennial

Habitat Coral cliffs (consisting of composite coral fragments) in coastal bushland.
Identification A herb or climber with pinnate leaves. The pink or purple flowers are scented and are borne on racemes that emerge from the leaf axils. They have a bell-like calyx with five lobes. The oblong seed pods are winged and contain up to 10 seeds.
Notes This climber can be used as a soil stabiliser, especially on sand dunes. It is grown as an ornamental.

Tephrosia villosa
PAPILIONACEAE FAMILY
80cm ◆ perennial/annual

Habitat Dry *Acacia-Commiphora* bushland; often on sandy soils.
Identification This herb has hairy stems and small, compound leaves, comprising up to 18 paired leaflets, each with a pointed tip. The pinkish-purple flowers are attached by short stalks to a central flower stem. Family Papilionaceae, to which this plant belongs, is part of the broader legume family whose members have a distinctive flower shape, with a large upper petal, two wing-like side petals and two fused lower petals. The pods are densely hairy, up to 5cm long and have an upcurved tip.
Notes This is a popular garden plant.

Trifolium rueppellianum
PAPILIONACEAE FAMILY
3cm ◆ annual

Habitat Damp open upland grassland; also found among shorter grasses.
Identification A small, creeping herb. The leaves comprise 3–4 leaflets joined at the base, with hairy margins and pale central markings **(1)**. The flowers vary from deep purple to pinkish-purple and form a rounded head up to 2cm across. The pods contain up to five seeds.
Notes Bees visit this and other *Trifolium* clover species to collect nectar.

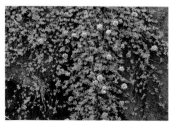

Trifolium semipilosum
PAPILIONACEAE FAMILY
6cm ◆ perennial

Habitat Open upland grassland.
Identification This tough, perennial herb is common in suitable habitat. Its stems creep along the ground, taking root at the nodes, and its compound leaves comprise three leaflets, each with a pale central line and a notched tip. The whitish-pink flowers are borne in rounded heads. Up to six seeds are held within each seed pod.
Notes An important source of nectar for bees.

Oxygonum sinuatum
POLYGONACEAE FAMILY
10cm ◆ annual

Habitat Open areas, often on disturbed ground. It is associated with a variety of vegetation types from *Acacia* bushland to dry forest margins.
Identification Widespread and common, this little annual has hairy stems and lanceolate leaves, which may be lobed and have a slight purple tinge along the margins and the rachis. Dainty flowers are borne close together on a single stem, and the seeds have 3–4 sharp points.
Notes The leaves are edible, with a tart taste similar to that of sorrel.

Polygala abyssinica
POLYGALACEAE FAMILY
10cm ◆ annual

Habitat Shallow soil overlying rock in *Acacia* bushland. Also occurs in open grassland.
Identification A small herb with soft, flat hairs on the purplish stems. The leaves are narrow and smooth. Mauve flowers appear at the nodes at the same time as the leaves. The sepals are equal in length to the petals.

Polygala sphenoptera
POLYGALACEAE FAMILY
10cm ◆ perennial/annual

Habitat At moderate altitude on rocky ground in dry *Acacia* bushland and open grassland.
Identification This delicate herb is a familiar sight in dry bushland after the rains. The leaves **(1)** are alternate, linear, narrow, and up to 4cm long. Pinkish-purple flowers on 6cm-long stalks emerge sideways from the main stem. Once pollinated, the wing-like petals turn cream with a purple margin.

Pentas lanceolata
RUBIACEAE FAMILY
1m ◆ perennial

Habitat The margins of moist upland forest, in association with *Podocarpus* and *Hagenia*; also found in the bamboo zone and in dry cedar-olive forest.
Identification A shrubby plant with shorts hairs on its stems, and ovate leaves with deeply indented veins. The flowers are carried in bunches at the tips of stems and vary in colour from very pale pink to mauve-purple.
Notes Attracts butterflies.

Solanum campylacanthum
(S. incanum (sensu **UKWF III***))*
SOLANACEAE FAMILY
1m ◆ perennial

Habitat Widespread in a range of habitats, often in disturbed areas; it is frequently considered a weed.

Identification This tough herb or small shrub has broad, soft, velvety leaves with wavy margins. Young leaves are often tinged deep purple. The flowers have five pale to dark purple petals, each with a slight central ridge (**1**). The round, variegated green fruits (**2**) measure up to 2cm and turn a distinctive bright yellow when ripe.

Notes Eland, kudu and elephant all enjoy eating the fruits. Their juice is said to be a cure for warts when applied daily. Chewing the taproot is a traditional treatment for chesty coughs.

Talinum portulacifolium
TALINACEAE FAMILY
1m ◆ perennial

Habitat At moderate altitude in various habitats, including rocky outcrops and moist and semi-arid *Acacia* bushland.

Identification This shallowly rooted plant has smooth stems and slightly fleshy, obovate leaves, which may have a purplish tinge along their margins. The bright, five-petalled flowers open only in the mornings and measure about 2cm across. They range from dark to pale purple. Soft, ovoid seed pods enclose the many small, shiny black seeds.

Lantana trifolia
VERBENACEAE FAMILY
1.5m ◆ perennial

Habitat At higher altitude in open grassland and along the margins of dry forest.
Identification A bushy shrub, widespread in its range, with hairy stems along which leaves are arranged in groups of three at regular intervals.

The leaves are broad at the base, narrow at the tip, with lightly toothed margins and a covering of soft hairs. The flowers may have yellow markings.
Notes Birds enjoy the small purple berries (1), which are also eaten by humans.

Siphonochilus kirkii
ZINGIBERACEAE FAMILY
12cm ◆ perennial

Habitat In shaded situations in coastal bushland, often in association with *Acacia*, *Annona*, *Zanthoxylum* and *Terminalia*, among others.
Identification This species arises from a short rhizome and its smooth, broad leaves appear along with the flowers. The flowering stem emerges from the basal leaves and carries several buds that open up one, or sometimes two at a time in succession. The papery petals have uneven margins, and there is a yellow nectar guide inside the lower petal.

Acanthus eminens
ACANTHACEAE FAMILY
2m ◆ perennial

Habitat The margins of upland forest, at high altitude.
Identification A large shrub that makes an attractive hedge. The broadly lanceolate leaves are up to 15cm long, with spine-tipped lobes. Large, dark blue to purple flowers are carried on a raceme measuring about 15cm. The flower bracts are covered in short, soft hairs (1).

Ajuga integrifolia (A. remota)
ACANTHACEAE FAMILY
40cm ◆ perennial

Habitat Open grassland and roadsides. Favours black cotton soils.
Identification A common, upright herb with greyish, toothed leaves clothed in soft hairs. The flowers, which are up to 0.9cm long, emerge in rows from the leaf axils (1).
Notes In traditional medicine, the leaves and stems are boiled to prepare an effective, but very bitter, decoction for treating malaria.

Barleria delamerei (*B. spinisepela*)

ACANTHACEAE FAMILY

15cm ◆ perennial

Habitat Sandy, well-drained soils in arid areas and in *Acacia* bushland.

Identification A very spiny, locally common herb with dark green, oval to elliptical leaves that have a sharply pointed apex. There are pinnate spines among the leaves (**1**). The lilac flowers, which emerge from the leaf axils, measure about 2.5cm in length, and the pods are woody capsules that split in half to release the seeds.

Notes Like most *Barleria* species, it is pollinated by hawk moths at night. In flower it makes a very pretty sight in dry bushland.

Blepharis edulis (*B. linarifolia*)

ACANTHACEAE FAMILY

6cm ◆ perennial

Habitat Open, sunny locations in semi-arid and desert areas; also, *Acacia-Commiphora* woodland up to 1,220m. Found on various soil types.

Identification Mostly prostrate, it creeps along, rooting at the nodes, and can cover large bare areas. The leaves are almost stalkless, linear and unevenly toothed (**1**), with small hairs on their upper surface. The flowers are blue, mauve or purple; the sepals have small spines (**2**).

Notes In semi-arid areas it provides fodder for camels, goats, donkeys and cattle when there is no grass. Also an important food for bees in dry areas.

Blepharis maderaspatensis
ACANTHACEAE FAMILY
20cm ◆ perennial

Habitat Dry *Acacia-Commiphora* bushland and grassland.
Identification A tall, rather straggly plant with upright stems. The leaves are arranged in whorls and are asymmetrical, with smooth margins. Solitary blue flowers 1.5cm long are borne in the leaf axils. The upper bracts are rounded, with recurved tips and strongly backward-curving bristles (1).
Notes An important forage plant for bees, especially in drier areas, where very few plants flower year-round.

Brillantaisia lamium
ACANTHACEAE FAMILY
2m ◆ perennial

Habitat Upland forest, from West Africa to Uganda; it has become naturalised in upland riverine vegetation in East Africa.
Identification A tall, erect plant with many branches that arise from the base of the stem. Its leaves are large and broad, with slightly wavy margins, and the 3cm-long flowers are borne in elongated panicles. The upper petal is pale purple and bears purple hairs, the lower lip is blue to dark purple. The sepals that protect the petals are covered in glandular hairs. (1)

Dyschoriste thunbergiiflora
ACANTHACEAE FAMILY
1m ◆ perennial

Habitat Dry, rocky areas and *Acacia-Commiphora* bushland.
Identification A rather woody shrub, with ovate, dark green leaves with a small point at the apex, and striking, blue to purple trumpet-shaped flowers with darker purple markings in the throat. The seed pod is a woody capsule.
Notes This is a horticulturally valuable species that can be planted as a shrub or trained into a hedge.

Hygrophila schulli
ACANTHACEAE FAMILY
80cm ◆ perennial

Habitat Coastal belt to upland areas, always close to water, such as swamps and streams.
Identification Widespread in its range, this upright plant has many squarish stems arising from the base. Whorls of leaves alternate with clusters of neatly arranged flowers, which vary in colour from mauve to white, with two yellow markings at the base of each petal. The leaves are covered in white glandular hairs. Sharp orange spines **(1)** emerge from the flower bracts. The leaves are lanceolate, with softly hairy margins.

Megalochlamys revoluta (*Ecbolium revolutum*)
ACANTHACEAE FAMILY
80cm ◆ perennial

Habitat Locally common in dry *Acacia-Commiphora* bushland. Favours semi-shaded positions and sandy soils.
Identification A small, shrub-like herb. The stems are pale grey, and the leaves are ovate, with rounded or pointed tips **(1)**. The inflorescence measures up to 1.2cm in length and has unusual overlapping bracts **(2)**. Each flower has three lower petals and one upper petal. Both the leaves and stems are clothed in soft hairs.
Notes Bees collect the pollen.

Ruellia patula
ACANTHACEAE FAMILY
20cm ◆ perennial

Habitat At moderate altitude, in shaded positions beneath trees or shrubs in dry bushland or on forest margins. Does not occur in desert or moorland areas.
Identification An upright herb with many branches. The leaves are ovate and slightly hairy, and the flowers are highly variable, reaching 3cm in length and ranging in colour from blue to pale pink or mauve. The petals have a deep central groove. The woody capsules split in half when dry, releasing their seeds.

Thunbergia petersiana
ACANTHACEAE FAMILY
1m ◆ perennial

Habitat Forest edges and high-altitude bushland. It is absent from dry *Acacia-Commiphora* bushland. Favours shaded positions.
Identification An upright herb that tends to clamber up shrubs and trees for support. The dull, hairless leaves are stalkless, broadly ovate, with slightly wavy margins and pointed tips. Unlike the related *T. holstiii*, this plant is not at all woody and its flowers are darker with a yellow throat, and slightly larger, measuring up to 6cm in length.

Caralluma arachnoidea
APOCYNACEAE FAMILY
20cm ◆ perennial

Habitat Hidden among clumps of grass in rocky areas, or protected by other plants such as *Sansevieria* species.
Identification A succulent herb with angular stems that branch from the base. The stems, which are up to 9cm long, are pale greenish-grey during the rains, but turn pale brown in the dry season, making this plant harder to spot at that time. Spider-like flowers (1) hang from the tips of the stems. They are variable, but generally deep purple with purple hairs on the petals.

Aponogeton abyssinicus
APONOGETONACEAE FAMILY
35cm ◆ annual

Habitat Seasonal pools during the rains. Occurs in various habitats at a range of altitudes, but is absent from very arid areas.
Identification An attractive water plant. The leaves are long, narrow and strap-like, up to 10cm in length, and float on the water surface. Flowers are borne in groups of two, each with 2–3 purple tepals. The vegetative parts shrivel when the water dries up.
Notes This is an attractive plant to add to a pond.

Sphaeranthus suaveolens
ASTERACEAE FAMILY
20cm ◆ perennial

Habitat Always close to permanent or seasonal water. Often found along with sedges at moderate altitude. It is absent from desert and moorland areas.
Identification A shrubby herb with winged stems **(1)**. The leaves are stalkless, lanceolate and irregularly toothed, and the purple flowers are borne in a compact, rounded head **(2)**.
Notes The leaves are aromatic. In some traditional communities women take advantage of their natural perfume by knotting the leaves into beaded necklaces.

Vernonia galamensis
ASTERACEAE FAMILY
1.5m ♦ perennial

Habitat Upland forest, where it grows in disturbed ground or along the margins of rivers and streams.
Identification This tall plant is often supported by other plants. It has glandular stems and hairy, elliptical leaves. There are pale green, leaf-like scales **(1)** on the bracts of the compact flowers, which can be pale blue or purple. A highly variable species, with up to four subspecies.
Notes The attractive flowers and densely hairy seed heads **(2)** are suitable for use in dried flower arrangements.

Cystostemon hispidus
BORAGINACEAE FAMILY
25cm ♦ annual

Habitat Volcanic soil in open Rift Valley grassland.
Identification This common, upright, Rift Valley herb has hairy, elliptical leaves carried in bunches of three or four. The pale blue flowers are alternately arranged and borne on pinkish flowering stalks **(1)** at the top of the stems. The plant is covered in soft white hairs **(2)** and bears brown nutlets shaped a bit like pyramids.

Echiochilon lithospermoides
BORAGINACEAE FAMILY
80cm ◆ annual

Habitat Dry, disturbed locations, especially roadsides and ditches. Favours black cotton and sandy soils.
Identification A locally common, upright, hairy herb with spiky, many-branched stems and a rough surface texture. The narrow grey-green leaves have stiff hairs and glands on their undersurface. The flowers may be blue, purplish or a mixture of both colours, and the fruits are hard, brownish nutlets (1).
Notes Many species of butterfly flock to this plant.

Lobelia fervens
CAMPANULACEAE FAMILY
15cm ◆ annual

Habitat Forest margins and grassland, mostly in shaded positions; often forms pure stands in sandy or shallow soil.
Identification This hairless, upright herb may cover large areas. It has narrow, alternating leaves with toothed margins and bears a profusion of blue flowers, each up to 2.5cm long, with three petals.

Lobelia gregoriana (L. deckenii)
CAMPANULACEAE FAMILY
3m ◆ **perennial**

Habitat Among moorland grasses in Kenya's Aberdare range.
Identification A tall, upright plant with a rosette of hairy leaves at its base and a tall, cylindrical flowering stem up to 2cm wide. The deep purple flowers are almost hidden in the large, leafy bracts of the inflorescence, which is broad at the base and tapers; the petals **(1)** are deep purple and have a large lower lip. There are short soft hairs within the corolla.

Lobelia telekii
CAMPANULACEAE FAMILY
4m ◆ **perennial**

Habitat Among tussock grasses on Mt Kenya, Mt Elgon and the Aberdares. More widespread than *L. gregoriana*.
Identification An intriguing plant with many narrow leaves at its base and a tall flowering spike that may attain over a metre in height. This spike is covered in what looks like a mass of feathers, but are actually bracts that protect the small purple-and-white flowers **(1)** (each up to 2.2cm long). The sepals are hairy.

Aneilema hockii
COMMELINACEAE FAMILY
20cm ◆ perennial

Habitat Among rocks close to seasonal streams in dry country.
Identification A fleshy herb with leafy stems that spread out on the ground, and upright flowering stems. The leaves are broadly elliptical, with wavy margins that may be purplish. The delicate, pale mauve flowers make this the most striking local *Aneilema*. They are up to 4cm in diameter and fragrant. The purple-and-green-striped sepals **(1)** are a key identifying characteristic. The seed capsules contain up to 12 seeds.

Commelina benghalensis
COMMELINACEAE FAMILY
60cm ◆ annual/perennial

Habitat Forest margins, bushland and disturbed habitats.
Identification A highly variable trailing herb that can attain 2m if supported, but otherwise creeps along the ground, rooting at the nodes. The leaves are spirally arranged, up to 3cm long, and slightly hairy. The spathe enclosing the flowers has white or orange marginal hairs **(1)**. Seeds are produced both above and below ground.
Notes Eaten as a vegetable in Uganda and used in traditional blessing ceremonies. It is also fed to rabbits and poultry and is revered by pastoralists, as it increases milk yield in sheep.

Commelina erecta
COMMELINACEAE FAMILY
75cm ◆ perennial

Habitat Dry bushland and grassland.
Identification A creeping or climbing herb that may attain 1m if supported. It has narrow, generally hairy, lanceolate leaves up to 3cm long. Like other *Commelina* species, its stems may be smooth or lightly hairy, which can make identification difficult. The pale blue flowers have three petals, including a central ribbon-like (1) petal. In hotter areas, the spathe (2) tends to be hairy.
Notes An important source of pollen for bees in dry areas.

Commelina forskaolii
COMMELINACEAE FAMILY
22cm ◆ perennial

Habitat Grassland and bushland.
Identification A small herb that forms tight clumps. Leafy, blue-tinged stems with purple markings (1) arise from the base and may be prostrate or trailing. The often grey-green leaves are alternate, about 3cm long, with wavy margins. The blue flowers have winged stamen filaments (2).

Cyanotis arachnoidea
COMMELINACEAE FAMILY
10cm ◆ perennial

Habitat Rocky outcrops at moderate altitude.
Identification A small herb with a rosette of leaves at its base and smaller, simple leaves along the flowering stem. The stem is often purple, as are the undersides of the leaves, and both stem and leaves are clothed in woolly hairs. The flowers have hairy styles, giving them a fluffy appearance.

Evolvulus alsinoides
CONVOLVULACEAE FAMILY
3cm ◆ annual/perennial

Habitat Sandy soils in dry, open bushland.
Identification A variable plant that tends to spread out close to the ground. The stems and leaves are clothed in long, silky hairs **(1)** and the leaves are linear and alternately arranged. Small, solitary, purplish-blue flowers up to 6cm across, with prominent white stamens, are borne on a short stalk and emerge from the leaf bases.
Notes With its small, very pretty flowers, this plant is a distinctive feature of dry areas in the region; it may be surprising to learn that it is a member of the morning glory family.

Jacquemontia tamnifolia
CONVOLVULACEAE FAMILY
1m ◆ **annual/perennial**

Habitat Margins of coastal forest; also, mudflats on the edges of permanent lakes.
Identification A delicate herb with heart-shaped, slightly hairy leaves. Striking blue flowers are borne in small bunches (cymes) clothed with soft hairs (1), and measure about 1cm in diameter.

Monsonia angustifolia
GERANIACEAE FAMILY
10cm ◆ **annual**

Habitat Open grassland.
Identification A small herb with narrow leaves. The margins are softly wavy, with a purplish tinge. The flowers have 4–5 pale mauve petals and are carried on stalks up to 2cm long. The sepals are softly hairy. When the upright seed pod dries out, it peels open, releasing the seeds.

Saintpaulia rupicola
GESNERIACEAE FAMILY
7cm ◆ perennial

Habitat Shaded positions on granite rock close to water, or in shallow, damp soil in coastal forest.
Identification The leaves of this small herb form a rosette. They are toothed, heart-shaped, up to 6cm in width and 5cm long, with a slightly hairy surface. Several flowers are carried on the flowering stalk, and the petals are up to 2cm wide. The lower petals are larger.
Notes This species is the likely ancestor of all African violet hybrids globally. Loss of habitat poses a serious threat, and few plants remain in the wild.

Streptocarpus caulescens
GESNERIACEAE FAMILY
13.5cm ◆ perennial

Habitat The margins of mountain streams and other moist, shaded locations. Seeds often land on and germinate in moss-covered trees.
Identification A brittle, trailing herb with rounded, fleshy leaves. Most parts of the plant are clothed in soft glandular hairs. Bears a profusion of pendent, tubular, deep violet flowers, each up to 1.8cm long.

Moraea stricta (M. thompsonii)

IRIDACEAE FAMILY

1m ◆ perennial

Habitat Damp, high-altitude grassland.
Identification A tall, pretty lily with
narrow, cylindrical leaves that appear at
the same time as the pale lilac flowers.
These are up to 5cm in width and
comprise three large petals marked with
yellow nectar guides (1), alternating
with three much smaller petals.

Nepeta azurea

LAMIACEAE FAMILY

75cm ◆ perennial

Habitat Upland grassland; also
roadsides at higher altitude.
Identification A tall herb that forms
large clumps. It branches from the
base, bearing narrow, toothed,
opposite leaves (1) with grey hairs
on the undersurface. Dense cymes (2)
of small flowers are carried in a
terminal inflorescence.
Notes Essential oil derived from this
plant is an effective mosquito repellent.

Plectranthus barbatus
LAMIACEAE FAMILY
4m ◆ perennial

Habitat Rocky areas at moderate to high altitude; also occurs around cultivated plots *(shambas)*, where it is grown as a hedge.

Identification In its natural habitat, harsh environmental conditions and browsers such as kudu keep this fleshy, aromatic plant quite small. However, when it is protected, it can become quite large and makes a useful hedge. The leaves have a broad base, a narrower tip, and toothed margins. The terminal inflorescences with pale blue to mauve flowers are up to 20cm long. Glandular hairs cover the flowering stems.

Plectranthus caninus
LAMIACEAE FAMILY
10cm ◆ perennial

Habitat Shallow soils on rocky ground in open grassland; often associated with *Acacia drepanolobium*.

Identification This locally abundant *Plectranthus* creeps along the ground, covering large areas. It has softly hairy stems and its leaves are wedge-shaped, slightly fleshy and also adorned with soft hairs. The upright flowering spike bears a compact inflorescence about 7cm long, from which just a few flowers emerge at a time. The upper bracts are pale purple tinged with mauve. All parts of the plant have a strong, slightly unpleasant smell when crushed.

Plectranthus montanus
LAMIACEAE FAMILY
3m ◆ perennial

Habitat Locally common in drier areas in *Acacia-Commiphora* bushland.
Identification A hairy trailing herb that may form dense stands. The leaves are succulent, shiny green and broadly ovate, with dentate margins. They are slightly aromatic when crushed. Pale mauve flowers are borne on a softly hairy, cylindrical raceme. Generally small, they may be a bit larger in some areas, and the stamens are always longer than the petals.

Plectranthus pseudomarrubioides
LAMIACEAE FAMILY
8cm ◆ perennial

Habitat Rocky ground in dry *Acacia* bushland at moderate altitude.
Identification A fleshy plant that often spreads out over large areas, making a good ground cover. The leaves are pale green, thick and rounded, slightly hairy, with toothed margins. They are aromatic when crushed. Bunches of flowers are borne at intervals along the stem. The sepals are woolly (1).

Notes The juice from the leaves is used as a traditional remedy for skin cancer. Some people also apply it to reduce the appearance of age spots.

Pycnostachys coerulea
LAMIACEAE FAMILY
30cm ◆ perennial

Habitat Swampy areas and the shores of freshwater lakes.
Identification When flowering, this small, branching herb is striking in its lakeshore habitat. It has squarish purple stems (1) and narrow, drooping leaves with toothed margins (2). Small blue flowers are carried in compact spikes at the tips of the stems. They are clothed in tiny glandular hairs.

Salvia merjamie
LAMIACEAE FAMILY
1m ◆ perennial

Habitat At higher altitude in areas of bare ground with volcanic soils.
Identification An upright herb with several stems emerging from a rosette of long, lobed leaves, each up to 10cm in length, with toothed margins (1). The leaves higher up on the stem are far smaller than those nearer the base. The bluish purple flowers have soft hairs in the throat and are borne in a compact raceme up to 20cm long.

Nymphaea nouchali
NYMPHAECEAE FAMILY
1m ◆ **perennial**

Habitat Permanent and seasonal water catchments, from the coastal belt up to nearly 1,800m.
Identification This aquatic lily requires a minimum water depth of 1m. It has potato-like roots, which hold it firmly in place, and its leaves are round, with smooth margins. The flowers are mauve or blue, up to 20cm in diameter, and an important source of pollen for bees. The rounded seed head is divided into sections packed with small, greyish seeds. This seed head sinks into the mud, where new plants germinate.
Notes People eat the rich, oily seeds. The roots, too, are edible when peeled.

Clitoria ternatea
PAPILIONACEAE FAMILY
4m ◆ **perennial**

Habitat Dry, hot bushland and the coastal belt. Usually comes up after good rains.
Identification A strikingly beautiful climber with variable pinnate leaves, each comprising 5–7 leaflets (**1**). The flowers are generally pale blue, but some may be almost white. They are borne in the leaf axils and measure up to 3cm in length. The flat seed pod is about 1cm long.

Lupinus princei
PAPILIONACEAE FAMILY
1m ◆ perennial

Habitat Locally common in grassland.
Favours volcanic soils. Often forms
pure stands.
Identification This leafy herb is very
conspicuous when flowering, as it
bears tall, upright flowering stems.
The flowers are blue with a pale yellow
centre. The leaves are palmate (1), pale
green above and softly hairy on the
undersurface.
Upward-pointing
pods (2) follow
the flowers.
Notes This plant
is pollinated by
carpenter bees.

Delphinium macrocentrum
RANUNCULACEAE FAMILY
70cm ◆ perennial

Habitat Moist rocky areas and
tussock grassland, at altitudes of
1,650–3,000m.
Identification A delicate, upright
plant with roughly circular, deeply
incised leaves (1). It carries many deep
blue, graceful flowers on a single
stem. The flowers have a rather stout,
upward-pointing spur (2).

Pentanisia ouranogyne
RUBIACEAE FAMILY
13.5cm ◆ perennial

Habitat Disturbed, open ground in dry grassland. Often along roads and in ditches. Favours sandy soils.
Identification A short herb that forms large clumps and has linear, grey-green leaves. The pale blue flowers measure about 2cm in diameter and have a hairy floral tube. They are densely clustered in rounded heads.
Notes This species is pollinated mainly by butterflies.

Craterostigma alatum
SCROPHULARIACEAE FAMILY
6cm ◆ perennial

Habitat Bushland and arid areas; always in shallow soil and full sun.
Identification A small, pretty herb that grows from a rhizome and has orange roots. It forms a rosette of broad leaves, which are smooth or lightly hairy, with toothed or entire margins. Small bright blue or purple flowers with yellow stamens are borne on upright stems, and the sepal tube has keel-like wings **(1)**.
Notes This plant, which emerges with the rains, is believed to herald a good rainy season.

Viola abyssinica
VIOLACEAE FAMILY
8cm ◆ perennial

Habitat Forests; favours deep shade, damp locations and loamy soils.
Identification A small, clump-forming, slightly hairy herb, with trailing stems that root at the nodes. The heart-shaped leaves have softly serrated, hairy margins and taper to a point. The flowers are up to 1.2cm long; the four whitish upper petals may be tinged with purple, the lower one is dark blue or violet.
Notes Attractive and delicate, this plant brightens up the dark forest floor. Ants feed on the seeds.

Siphonochilus brachystemon
ZINGIBERACEAE FAMILY
10cm ◆ perennial

Habitat Exclusive to the coastal belt.
Identification An upright plant with long, strappy leaves. The stalkless flowers are produced at ground level and have four lobes: the lower lobes are large, while the upper lobes are much smaller and form a V-shape. There are two yellow spots at the centre of each pale blue flower. The fruits are red.

GLOSSARY

appressed: lying flat against (e.g. hairs on a leaf)

bract: a small, modified leaf or scale, with a flower(s) in its axil

capitate: forming or shaped like a head or dense cluster

cladode: a flat, leaf-like stem

entire: without notches or indentations

epiphyte: a plant that grows on another plant

exserted: protruding out (like the stamens of the corolla)

herb: a seed-bearing plant that lacks a woody stem and dies after flowering

hirsute: covered with long, stiff hairs

inflorescence: the entire flower head, consisting of the stems, stalks, bracts and flowers

lateritic: rust-red soils that contain iron and aluminium

node: the region of a stem from which the leaves emerge, often forming a slight swelling

obovate: ovate with a narrower end at the base

pollinia: a mass of pollen grains produced by each anther lobe in some flowers

sepal: the typically green, leaf-like parts of the calyx of a flower, which enclose the petals

REFERENCES AND FURTHER READING

Agnew, ADQ. 2013. *Upland Kenya Wild Flowers and Ferns*. Nature Kenya, The East Africa Natural History Society. Nairobi.

Beentje, HJ. 1994. *Kenya Trees, Shrubs and Lianas*. National Museums of Kenya. Nairobi.

Blundell, M. 1982. *The Wild Flowers of Kenya*. Collins. London.

Royal Botanic Gardens (series). 1940–2012. *Flora of Tropical East Africa*. Kew Publishing. Kew.

Sapieha, T. 2008. *Wayside Flowers of East Africa*. Sapieha. Nairobi.

INDEX TO SCIENTIFIC NAMES